Contexts

for Learning

Institutional Strategies for Managing Curricular Change Through Assessment

Editor Bruce Keith

United States Military Academy

NEW FORUMS PRESS INC.

Stillwater, Okla. U.S.A.

NEW FORUMS PRESS INC.

Published in the United States of America
by New Forums Press, Inc.
1018 S. Lewis St.
Stillwater, OK 74074
www.newforums.com

Copyright © 2004 by New Forums Press, Inc.

Library of Congress Cataloging-in-Publication Data Pending

This book may be ordered in bulk quantities at discount from New Forums Press, Inc., P.O. Box 876, Stillwater, OK 74076 [Federal I.D. No. 73 1123239]. Printed in the United States of America.

International Standard Book Number: 1-58107-086-1

Contents

Preface

I have been involved with institutional and program level assessments long enough to conclude with confidence that the vast majority of conversations on assessment center on the collection of evidence. Whatever most people think about assessment—strategy, practice, accountability, improvement—ultimately the conversation comes back to data. These conversations are not limited to one particular group of individuals; indeed, I've encountered these discussions at conference meetings held by the American Association of Higher Education, the Association of Institutional Research, the American Sociological Association, the American Association for Engineering Education, as well as other venues including the National Science Foundation and as a team member on various institutional and program accreditation reviews.

I contend that a focus on data collection is not inherently misguided; rather, such a focus is simply narrowly conceived. Although the collection of evidence is an important part of any assessment plan, it is not necessarily the most important component of the plan. Instead, the process an organization employs for the purpose of managing change provides a framework that offers meaning to the evidence collected. This process involves a coherent framework, developed within a particular institutional context and culture, which allows for the management of curricular change. Indeed, process is central to the way institutions manage change. Toward this end, assessment is all about process—basic assumptions about the mission and direction of the institution, political and intra-institutional dynamics between and among faculty and administration, collaboration and consensus-building, and the collection of evidence—for the sole purpose of managing change meaningfully within the institution.

The purpose of this book is to re-center the conversation on assessment from one focused on assessment-as-evidence to an alternative perspective that emphasizes assessment-as-process. Questions and discussions on assessment that surface routinely in various venues must ultimately come back to a emphasize process, with a particular focus on an institution's context and culture. One of the great frustrations often encountered by assessment practitioners in higher education is the realization that published models are not easily imported into their own institutional environments. In working with assessment, they learn that their strategy must be tailored to the specific parameters—context and culture—of their own institutions. This realization requires them to design and implement an assessment plan within the established mechanisms (process) employed by their institution to manage change. This suggestion, although intuitively obvious, is a subject often overlooked in conversations about assessment through public dialogues and professional publications.

Why Understand Assessment-as-Process?

In directing attention toward assessment as a process, I am explicitly suggesting a need to focus more closely on institutional contexts for student learning. This requires one to look within schools in an effort to understand how the successful reform strategies employed by those schools are related to their contextual and cultural frameworks. What is proven to work at one school may not work at another because of differences in mission, the faculty's orientation toward students or teaching, patterns of collaboration, administrative structures, and basic underlying assumptions about how change ought to occur in the institution. Our understanding of assessment-as-process draws attention to the importance of intra-organizational dynamics in managing change strategies. Indeed, I offer five reasons why we collectively need to understand assessment-as-process. *A focus on process is necessary because it draws attention to institutional context.* Institutions vary from one another with regard to their vision and constituencies. Institutions also vary in terms of their socialization practices of new members, patterns of information and communication flow, technologies, and leadership. The patterns of interaction that faculty maintain with their students will fluctuate along a continuum between a student-centered focus and one oriented around their research. Thus, organizational efforts at implementing an assessment plan will require attention to these contextual factors if an assessment plan is to be understood and valued within an institutional environment.

A focus on process emphasizes the importance of institutional culture. Change strategies, such as the design and implementation of a comprehensive assessment plan, require that they be developed and articulated within recognizable patterns of shared learning. Cultures provide organizations with structural stability and integration, which implies a history of stable, shared experiences. As such, culture provides members with a shared experience about the value of the organization and the structured processes through which members work together to achieve commonly understood outcomes. An assessment plan oriented toward process rather than evidence operates within an institutional culture that is more effective in legitimating any recommendations derived from a utilization of the plan.

A focus on process, in illuminating cultural assumptions, serves as an important mechanism for understanding an institution's resistance to change. Organizational leaders who do not understand their institution's culture risk having the culture manage them. The successful management of organizational change requires decision-makers to understand why particular changes have been effectively implemented in the past while other proposed changes have been effectively shelved. To the extent that cultures represent stability and integration, organizational changes may be viewed as a threat to the culture. Members will likely resist change strategies until they become managed within a familiar process. Institutional assessment, as one such change strategy, needs to grow out of the shared experiences of its members lest it be openly challenged by them. Toward this end, assessment must be seen as an integrated process and not as an accessory to that process.

A focus on process underscores the relevance of collaboration, particularly between and among faculty and administration. Organizational leaders who manage assessment as a process within the recognizable frameworks of an institution do so within established patterns of collaboration and communication. The manner in which faculty interact with one another and the administration represents a history of patterned relations. The successful assessment plan must tap into these established processes of collaboration if faculty and administrators are to effectively use the plan to improve the institution's academic programs.

A focus on process provides institutional leaders, who move from one institution to another, with a common understanding of how to manage institutional reform. The successes enjoyed by one institution may represent the dismal failures of another. This happens because organizational leaders, who have enjoyed success at one institution, fail to propose change within the organizational history of their new charge. To wit, they fail precisely because they attempt to import what worked elsewhere into their current environment. The successful management of organizational assessment, as one type of reform, is likely to depend on the development of a plan within the contextual parameters of an institution. Leaders who relocate from one institution to another are more likely to succeed in the implementation of comprehensive assessment plans when these plans are "home grown" with the contextual "nutrients" available to them in their new environments.

Who Should Read This Book?

This book is written for several distinct audiences. In bringing together the perspectives of faculty, administrators, and practitioners, I have tried to balance academic rigor with practical application. Administrators will find value in learning how their counterparts at other institutions have successfully managed the implementation of assessment plans. Faculty, as scholars, will hopefully find that the essays further the professional dialogue on assessment. Faculty, as practitioners, will find value in the utility of the essays as practical suggestions worthy of consideration in their own efforts to manage assessment locally. Finally, students of higher education and organizational behavior will gain insights into the dynamics of higher educational reform through exposure to several new and relevant institutional case studies.

Overview of the Contents

I became familiar with many of the contributors of this book through my work with the Middle States Commission on Higher Education, the institutional accreditation association for the Middle States region in the United States. I selected the contributors for this book in one of two ways. First, at Ed Neal's request, I served as a guest editor for an issue of the *Journal of Staff, Program, and Organizational Development* in 1999 (volume 16, number 4), a New Forums Press publication. Four of the nine chapters in this book are reprinted from that issue, which focused on assessing the effectiveness of higher educational institutions. All but one of the remaining contributors were selected for inclusion in this book based on their presentations to participants at annual conferences of the Middle States Commission on Higher Education. Second, I sought contributions that highlighted the assessment strategies at various types of institutions, from the community college (Baltimore County), baccalaureate degree (Kings College, United States Military Academy), master's degree (SUNY-Oneonta), and doctoral degree (Penn State). Moreover, I sought to include a contribution from an institution whose primary constituency included nontraditional students (Empire State). These contributions reflect the assessment processes employed by institutions that vary rather dramatically in terms of the contexts, cultures, and mission statements. However, I felt that the text was not complete without balancing these various perspectives against the standards established by the regional accreditation board—in this case, the Middle States Commission on Higher Education. Therefore, I sought to include a contribution from Middle States. This book includes contributions from distinctly different institutions within a single accreditation region as well as a contribution about accrediting learning, which was written by representatives from the accreditation board.

In underscoring the importance of contexts for learning, this book focuses on assessment within institutional environments. The lead essay by James Ratcliff provides an overview of assessment in diverse learning communities. Henry Linck offers us a detailed examination of assessment within a community college. Mitch Nesler draws attention to use of the Baldrige criteria as an effective strategy employed by a non-traditional academic institution. George Forsythe and Bruce Keith discuss the framework for assessment at a specialized baccalaureate degree-granting institution. Donald Farmer emphasizes the importance of course-embedded assessment strategies in moving an institution from summative to formative methodologies. Fred Volkwein underscores the value of assessment in the major within a large research university. Each of these essays discusses assessment within specific types of institutional contexts. The final three essays focus on assessment as process. Bruce Keith and James Forest illustrate how institutional leaders must be attentive to environment, vision, administrative support, collaboration, and professional development to effectively manage organizational change. Armand LaPotin and Carolyn Haessig apply John Kotter's eight stage process to an baccalaureate and masters-level degree-granting institution as a model for evolving informed faculty feedback in change strategies. MaryAnn Baenninger and Jean Morse speak to the standards for accrediting learning that are applied to the institutions highlighted throughout this book. Taken together, the essays showcase the importance of assessment-as-process within specific institutional contexts.

These essays, when read as a set, generate six common themes. First, efforts to continuously improve programs and ensure accountability require that curriculum design and assessment strategies must necessarily be integrated. Second, the successful integration of such strategies will require faculty and administrators to work in concert with one another. Third, while models of curriculum design and assessment have common components, they will ultimately be unique to each institution based on a distinct culture, history, and mission; hence, an emphasis should be placed on student learning rather than institutional comparisons. Fourth, the process through which assessment data are gathered is often as important as the outcomes themselves, giving all participants a sense of ownership in a process that is tailored to a specific context. Fifth, multiple indicators gathered at multiple time points are critical if institutions are to offer evidence that they actually add value to students' learning experiences. Sixth, students must be actively engaged as learners rather than remain passive recipients of knowledge. Taken together, the essays offer a forum intended to contribute to the important and ongoing discussions on the topic of program quality among higher educational institutions.

Acknowledgements

This book is the culmination of efforts from several individuals. First and foremost, Ed Neal served as a source of continual support and patience throughout the writing of this book. He originally asked me to serve as a guest editor for the *Journal of Staff, Program, and Organizational Development* and then, upon the completion of that issue, suggested that I might want to consider expanding that focus into a book-length manuscript. Without his support, this book would not have materialized. Second, Doug Dollar, editor of New Forums Press, has been extraordinarily supportive of this initiative, finding value in an ongoing conversation about assessment. Third, Barney Forsythe has, throughout the past seven years, served as both a source of inspiration and guidance. Fourth, my family—Kate, Barbara, and Mary—have provided the support necessary to remain attentive to my research agenda. And last but not least, my gratitude extends to the contributors of this text, who have provided insights and a framework for continuing our conversation on managing contexts for learning.

Bruce Keith
West Point, New York
December 2003

Dedicated to my parents, Donald and Elizabeth Keith

Who helped me to learn to teach myself.

The Rudder and the Sail: Assessment for Staff, Program, and Organizational Development

James L. Ratcliff
The Pennsylvania State University

In higher education generally, and community colleges in particular, it is common to think of assessment primarily as part of the diagnostic testing, advising, and placement services that students initially encounter upon enrollment. Increasingly, students enter college with a vast variety of backgrounds, experiences, and abilities. Assessment has been the process wherein students with specific learning needs or problems are referred to the appropriate developmental or remedial classes or services. But the assessment plans and programs called for today are much broader in scope and time frame than this. Policy makers, citizens, and parents want to know what has been the added value or contribution made by the college to students' growth and development of knowledge, skills and abilities. Impelling these reforms is more than merely an increased call for accountability. It asks for a new outlook on the part of staff, for a clear tie between program and student learning, and for a reorientation in the way the college organization does its business and makes its decisions (Ratcliff & associates 1995). It creates new challenges and new opportunities. Driving these changes is the fact that knowledge itself is exploding in growth. We need only reflect on the number of new fields coming to higher education over the past half century-from women's studies to computer science-to recognize this explosion. Further, if one reflects on how much a program in secretarial science or in biological science has changed over the three decades, one begins to see what pressures the academic programs have been under. This pressure, while large, is incremental in nature. Each year faculty are asked to cram more knowledge, skills, and abilities into overly-packed courses of study.

Yet new practices in pedagogy and instructional technology tell us that a curriculum piled higher and deeper is not necessarily a more effective one. Carefully crafted articulation agreements, 2 + 2 programs, and partnerships with the K-12 system do allow more coordination, sequencing, and refining of educational programs. However, the primary challenge remains - selecting what to teach *which students when and how.* Basic questions regarding how to improve and engage students, how to give sufficient time-on-task to learn key concepts and skills, and how to employ the latest in instructional technology and design beg for a better way to develop educational programs. Attendant pressures for curricular change come from new skill areas in information literacy, computer and media technologies, and from new partnerships with other sectors of education, the business community, and the diverse communities served.

Not only has knowledge exploded, but increasingly, jobs are more likely to require some form of higher education. At the beginning of the last century, research on colleges was tied to the traditional professions (theology, law, medicine) and only a small fraction of the population entered higher education. Today nearly 60 percent of all high school graduates will seek some form of higher education (U.S. Department of Education, 1996a). The sheer number of high school graduates is rising, and an increasing number of them expect to attend some form of postsecondary education. Estimates suggest that upwards of 70 percent will be at our doors within the decade (U.S. Department of Education, 1996b), and these estimates do not take into account our current efforts to improve in the quality of K12 and higher education programs. Clifford Adelman (1998) has argued that if K-12 school reform is only partially successful, it will send an additional 5 percent of high school graduates to college. And if we are successful in colleges and universities in reducing attrition, the combined effect may place as many as 1.7 million additional students into our higher education system! (Adelman 1998)

Governments increasingly view higher education as a benefit or right of citizenship. While community colleges were founded on the principal of low cost, easy access, and opportunity regardless of prior academic ability, government has played a key role in the expansion of college-going rates. State and federal grants and loans have also been expanded, the GI benefits have been extended to the national guards of the various states, and Peace Corps, Teacher Corp., Americorps, and America Reads all stimulate enrollment growth in their own way. All this puts greater pressure on colleges to provide better education to more student, more quickly, and most cost-efficiently.

Increasingly we are being asked to provide better programs in short amounts of instructional time at lower costs. States are turning to policies to ration or eliminate developmental and remedial education. In California and Florida, the community colleges are asked to absorb students requiring such assistance; states seek to limit the time a student can spend in college, trying to reduce the number of students reenrolling in development, remedial, or basic job skills programs (Institute for Higher Education Policy 1998). Such pressures, in effect, require colleges to work better, quicker, and cheaper. It not only asks us to set goals for our colleges that truly strengthen the organization, but also calls for a more accurate compass to chart our course.

In this milieu, assessment becomes a mechanism that allows us, as educators, to determine whether students have acquired the knowledge, skills, and abilities necessary to participate in specific aspects of society. Assessment takes teachers and colleges beyond the process of awarding grades and credits to identify the extent to which the goals of the educational program are sufficiently manifest in the student with demonstrable levels of competence necessary to engage in those realms of society predominated by the college-educated and the college graduate. Assessment becomes our social rudder in a world of rapidly changing knowledge, exploding diversity of student backgrounds, interests, and abilities, and expanding societal demands to prepare increasing proportions of the population for key social, economic, and political roles. Without the rudder of assessment, the colleges cannot easily maintain their course in such a complex environment. And without such a sail, students cannot readily gain timely and useful information that will enable them to persist, progress, and perform in their educational program. Assessment may be invaluable to colleges in better fulfilling their social role and to students in gaining better focus and direction in their learning; assessment offers a new, more accurate and useful avenue to determining educational quality.

Quality — What Is It, Really?

Quality at the institutional level is most often determined by simple reputation. The oldest and most distinguished of colleges and universities - Harvard, Berkeley, Michigan, Grinnell, Swathmore, Bennington, Reed are presumed to provide superior education because they attract many of the best and brightest students and because their graduates attain positions of highest responsibility in government and society. Yet, as the higher education system grows in size and complexity, reputation applies to only a few of the institutions within the system. Further, it is not clear whether the success of the students graduating from these institutions is due to the quality of instruction or their native abilities as students. If an institution accepts only the more able and intelligent of high school graduates, then their graduates will no doubt be intelligent and able regardless of the quality of their programs.

A second common means of determining quality is to examine the amount of resources given to an institution of higher education. The more the institution has to spend, the higher the quality of faculty, of research, of instruction, of facilities, and of service it is reasoned. Institutions like John Hopkins University and the Massachusetts Institute of Technology (as well as Berkeley, Harvard, and the like), rank very high in the proportion of federal grant support for research. Annually, the *Chronicle of Higher Education* ranks states on the per capita expenditures for higher education. While resources do matter to educational quality, they have a direct impact on the quality of student learning when they are spent on improving instruction and when they are spent wisely. Further, all the enhancements in the world are not going to improve the teaching / learning process without engaging the faculty, the academic program, and the student. Not surprisingly, research suggests there is little direct relationship between institutional expenditures and the quality of student learning. Increasingly, magazine rankings of the quality of institutions and programs are being used as indicators of quality. As the proportion of the population who goes to higher education increases, the need to know which institutions offer superior programs and services drives public interest in such ranking schemes. But again, research has called into question the relationship between institutional quality rankings and student learning (see, e.g., Keith 1999).

A fourth way of determining quality is to evaluate the achievement of students in their programs and to evaluate the teaching, research, and service productivity of faculty as indicators of institutional and programmatic quality. Assessment of student learning and institutional effectiveness has become common criteria in the accreditation and self-study processes employed in the United States. While reputation, resources, and ranking rely on often externally-defined inputs to the educational process, assessment relates to and relies on staff, program, and organizational effectiveness as determined by the extent to which students learn, progress, persist, and attain their educational aims.

And What Is Assessment, Exactly?

By assessment, we mean a way of describing student learning to identifiable audiences for clearly articulated reasons. Assessment is the process of defining, selecting, designing, collecting, analyzing, interpreting, and using information to increase students' learning and development. Assessment is seen as a process that includes discussions about what should be assessed and how information will be used, not just the hands-on testing of students (Marchese 1987). Assessment can produce information useful for *communication and decision making:* for students to decide how to improve their learning, for faculty to decide how to plan more effective instruction, for academic leaders to decide how to construct more effective programs. Research suggests that assessment can be valuable for improved communication and decision-making when the principles of good feedback are followed: the assessment information should be in such a form that it can facilitate improvement in student learning and/or program effectiveness, and the information should be received at a time when some actions can be taken to improve learning and effectiveness (Ratcliff & associates 1995).

Four reasons are generally given for integrating assessment of students and programs into the quality assurance program of the college. First, to provide international referencing of student learning as a basis for global cooperation and competition. Second, to reduce the bureaucracy and regulation, and, in exchange, to expect higher education to measure its outcomes. Third, to clarify and give direction to higher education; to give greater cohesion and coordination to programs and services. Fourth, to improve the levels, types and extent of student learning. Each of these reasons for assessment and evaluation may be seen as complementary or contradictory. For example, the second and third items may be contradictory as a higher education system moves from state steerage to state coordination. Increased regulation of programs and institutions may be needed at the outset to establish an assessment and evaluation system, but the creation of such a system may ultimately call for the reduction of direct intervention, regulation, and direction by the state in favor of self-regulation and self evaluation (Neave & van Vught 1994). The reasons for implementing an evaluation and quality assurance mechanism thus may serve the dual masters of accountability and improvement.

Today, most efforts and quality assurance engage both accountability and improvement models. What is and is not seen as a quality program or curriculum is very much the result of educational philosophy, beliefs, values, and normative positions (Barnett 1992; Fuhrmann and Grasha 1983; van Vught 1994). Quality is thus both a personal and social construct. Just as it is the cinematographer's challenge not to replicate life and story, but to bring to the audience vicariously to new perspectives, imagination and reflections through the art itself, the faculty in developing a curricular program create a representation of knowledge, culture, scholarship and perspective that allows for students of various backgrounds, interests and abilities to experience discovery and inquiry. To the extent that the faculty create the curriculum as an atomistic assemblage of single courses, lectures, and seminars, quality becomes established implicitly rather than explicitly. It becomes embedded in the various values and expectations of individual academic staff. Implicit assumptions about quality are unspoken ones, however; they give little guidance to students in learning improvement and provide little common ground among academic staff as to the outcomes of the educational program.

Assessing in a Diverse Learning Community

Through assessment, it is possible to gauge how well a distributional design, a core curriculum, or a modified system of prescribed courses, course clusters, and capstone experiences (Jones & Ratcliff 1991; White 1994; Reardon & Ramaley 1996; Wright 1996) serves each of several salient subgroups of students enrolling at your institution. What is needed is a new wave of educational reform wherein basic institutional requirements reflect the variation in student learning and the clear assessment of curricular goals upon admission, progress through their programs, upon graduation, transfer, or entrance into the workforce (Ratcliff & associates

1995). In moving toward this goal, a better gauge is needed to guide undergraduate education deliberations regarding quality and coherence. Assessment can be that gauge.

Criteria used in assessing educational programs should be broad, including (a) content learning, (b) cognitive development, (c) attitudes and motivation toward learning, and (d) basic persistence to degree completion. Given the diversity of learning that occurs in a college, undergraduate education assessment criteria must be broad enough to include all the major types of learning imparted by the institution, the state, and the nation. Therefore, because assessment is a new and imperfect science, curriculum and assessment committees should not presume that any one set of measures of student learning will capture all content, all forms of cognitive development, or all values and frames of reference a student may gain from her or his collegiate experience (Wright 1996).

To monitor attainment of multiple purposes requires multiple measures. Assessing oral and written communication skills a common general education goal - illustrates the point. There are simply no paper and pencil tests, papers, or projects that will assess a student's ability to make effective oral presentations. Likewise, it is impossible to assess students' writing skills by listening to them speak - multiple measures are required to assess both skills effectively. The range of cognitive development imparted in the college ranges from basic communication and computational skills to higher order reasoning abilities, such as creative thinking and problem-solving (Ratcliff & associates 1995). To describe student cognitive development, multiple measures are needed to paint the full spectrum of enhanced student capacities. So long as we use a limited array of measures in assessing student learning, the connection between undergraduate education curriculum and student learning will remain tangential. While an expansive array of measures is desirable, it need not be limitless. The number of criteria used can be deter-

---

mined by the number, breadth and depth of curricular aims posed by the undergraduate education curricular goals.

Assessing the Gap in Performance

Research has provided a variety of models to understand how to bring about change in organizations (see, e.g., Bolman & Deal 1991; Lindquist 1996; Morgan 1986). While no model explains all aspects of educational change or provides a blueprint for bringing it about, all rely to some degree on the concept of the performance gap. The performance gap concept suggests that change will be undertaken when individuals see a gap between current conditions and desired outcomes that is sufficiently large enough to motivate them to change. If the college staff or leaders do not believe that a sufficient gap exists, then current practices are likely to prevail. In short, without a gap in system performance, there will be no motive to change. Students are unlikely to change their learning strategies until they see a gap between their current efforts and expected levels of performance, and we are unlikely to alter our programs and services unless we know where they are working (and for whom) and where they are not.

Implicit in the concept of the performance gap is the need for some means of assessing current performance. However, since the goals and purposes of colleges and educational programs are often ambiguous and difficult to assess, few institutions have employed the performance gap directly as a conceptual basis for change (Lindquist 1996). Since the identification of a gap in performance rests upon some means of determining the current state of performance, quality assessment becomes both an end and a means. That is, as the means and methods for assessing the quality of different aspects of college operations improves, assessment directors, institutional planners, academic administrators, and curriculum committees become more inclined to use quality assessment as a means to determining gaps in performance. As a result, the use of assessment will rise with its proven utility in measuring quality in higher education. The largest hurdle is getting it started.

Targeting Improved Learning

What does the conversation about quality and assessment mean for staff, program, and organizational development? First, while there is no absolute definition of quality, there are individual definitions of quality reflected in single courses and single services rendered by individual staff across a campus. To assess the effectiveness of the student learning experience, there needs to be campus-wide discussions - targeted and substantive - about what constitutes a quality learning experience (see, e.g., Farmer 1999). For example, if a college has an education goal of enhancing students' ability to communicate effectively orally and in writing then the discussion needs to be focused there. Such targeting will counteract the tendency to assume that all staff have comparable expectations about what are the speaking and writing skills of the graduates of diploma, certificate, and degree programs. A substantive discussion will be guided by what people have written about effective speech and writing skills. Effective communication skills may be context specific, that is, they may be different in nursing than in either business or automotive programs.

And what if the college has no general education goals? It is not uncommon for a college to have stated requirements for general education but no clear explanation of why those requirements have been established. A college may, for example, specify that a student needs to take 15 credits in physical and life sciences but may not explain why. In a community college setting, for example, when I talk with faculty and ask why the goal is present, the answer is invariably "to transfer." Yes, that may be an intermediate goal, and one can say, "We require 15 credits because four-year colleges and universities in our area require 15 credits." However, this tells neither the student nor the fellow faculty members why one would study the physical and life sciences and what one should expect to learn from such study. It does not specify what level of learning is appropriate for student achievement nor what is possibly gained from such study. It is not a student learning *outcome*. Students progress, perform, and persist better when they know where they are headed we all do for that matter. Fundamental first steps in assessing student learning are (a) to state assessable goals, (b) to identify and specify the leading experiences that will assist students in attaining those goals, and, (c) to articulate the criteria and level of attainment for each area of learning. Too often we stop at specifying requirements and do not examine what type and level of learning we expect from the educational program. Students do find it easier when they know the purpose of the 15 credits. For example, an appropriate goal statement might be "Students will understand scientific terms, concepts and theories, and will formulate empirically-testable hypotheses." With such statements, faculty, staff, and programs have something to work toward and to communicate to students, helping them better understand what they will gain from their own learning efforts.

Is quality defined by attainment of predetermined standards or is it the development of the personal and intellectual powers of imagination, creation, enterprise and empowerment? In reality, the question so often posed is a false dichotomy. A quality program must attend to the developmental needs of individual students; otherwise, only a fraction of the current population will benefit from the educational program. At the same time, there must be clear standards for the educational program to guarantee its integrity and effectiveness from dilution. If clear standards are lacking then the college's capacity to develop talent and expertise needed by the society is not assured. Good teachers and able students alone will not ensure that learning takes place (Ratcliff & associates 1995). Clear definitions of who can benefit from a college or university education are needed on admission, at the time(s) of transfer between institutions, on graduation, and as students enter the workforce. But how can such clear definitions be reconciled with what we know about the development of creative talents, analytic skills, entreprenuerialism and empowerment in students? That question may be best addressed through an analogy. As we board a commercial airliner, we want pilots who are fully competent to operate the planes. We want individuals who will rigorously review the checklists of aircraft readiness for takeoff. Here the compliance with standards of practice may mean life or death. Similarly, once airborne, we want those same pilots to use their creative judgments in coping with bad weather, air turbulence, and other unexpected and unpredictable events. During a blinding snow and ice storm, we do not want those pilots to take out their manuals and go over their checklists! Quality educational programs have criteria, standards, methods and measures for determining the level knowledge, skills and abilities required. They also have provisions for students to develop and demonstrate their imaginative and creative talents for which a predictable, standard outcome would be a constraint on creativity, initiative, and industry. What constitutes quality is heavily determined by educational philosophy; within our colleges, several philosophies operate simultaneously, confusing and confounding the task of establishing and conducting assessments and program reviews to determine the merits of particular higher education programs. Then too, while quality assurance may focus on institutional or programmatic attributes, an outcomes orientation to quality assurance implies the gathering of evidence regarding the growth and development of student abilities as well as the resultant competence of graduates of the program.

The Rudder and the Sail: Assessment and Organizational Change

In this article, I have argued that assessment is the rudder to guide and sail to propel faculty, program, and organizational development. This argument rests on the assumption that organizations are cultures. As Bensimon (1990, p. 77) notes: "To view the institution as a cultural entity is to see it as a system of shared meanings, maintained by symbolic processes" Seen in this light, "organizational culture is the glue that holds the institution together" (Rhoads & Tierney 1992, p. 5).

From a cultural perspective, organizational development is conceived with, proceeds from, and resonates to the college organizational culture. Assessment can provide, for example, evidence of where students are succeeding and where they experience difficulty within the context of the educational goals and pedagogical practices of the college (see, e.g., Farmer 1999). How that information is disseminated, discussed, and used as a basis for development should be determined within the context where students, staff, and administrators interact with one another. If half of the learning gains of students in their first years of college are attributed to out of class experiences (Ratcliff & associates 1995), then what forums for discussions are available for student services and academic affairs professionals meaningfully to interact and explore alternatives for improvement based on the assessment information? Traditional distinctions between units, such as those between student and academic affairs, and "organizational saga" shape and constrain change within institutions of higher education (Clark 1972), and are the "stuff" of its history (Shafer 1974).

Leaders assume special, often *ad hoc* roles, within cultures. Negotiation of diverse views, interests, and needs within a system of shared meaning becomes critical to progress and change. Similar negotiation between internal and external constituencies is also necessary. Often, such negotiation is seen as a process of bringing compliance to the previously established or presidentially proclaimed college mission and goals. Differences within the community college are to be resolved, minimized, or neutralized through consensus, compliance, or coercion processes. Such a perspective on leadership views *the absence of tension as a precondition to progress.* It may be less arduous for a leader to subsume differences and diversity within the organization, but it limits the extent to which the leader will tap the talent within the organization (Montgomery 1995).

Yet, it is ironic that viewed from the leader-follower paradigm, *the absence of tension is the basis for change.* An alternative perspective sees the diversity of views, experience, and interests as tensions that propel the college community to explore new directions. Contradiction and conflict are normal facets of an organizational culture, and are essential characteristics of the change process in the engaged, democratic college community. The role of a change agent is transformed from resolving differences, seeking compromise, and minimizing conflict to one of embracing diversity as the basis of empowerment, enterprise, ingenuity and change. So, if assessment, in its rudder function, points to the gap between current and desired levels of student development and attainment, it follows that the sources of that gap and the strategies to narrow it will be as diverse as the talent and imagination of the staff. Effective leadership for programmatic and organizational change to promote and enhance student learning must embrace and empower the naturally-occurring tensions resulting from diverse views on the causes, consequences, and courses of action suggested by assessment data.

For change to become embedded within the organization, members must envision the organization, their role within the organization, and the role of others in a new and innovative manner. Assessment can point the way to connections between disparate campus units, leaders, and programs in contributing to the attainment of learning aims (see, e.g., La Potin and Haessig 1999). To assess students upon entry, at various stages of their educational program, upon completion, and in the workforce, as suggested by Forsythe and Keith (1999), will require the cooperation of admissions, faculty, placement, and alumni offices. Working together they can plan assessments at key points in the students' career to profile their growth, development and educational attainment. To do this, those units need to be brought together, engage in constructive dialogue, and formulate alternative courses of action, fostering new forms of staff, program, and organizational development.

Assessment of student learning is rapidly replacing institutional or programmatic reputation, the calculation of resources devoted to institution or program, or any published ranking as the primary basis for determining the quality of the student learning experience. Assessments should ask not whether a program is good or bad, but which groups of students seem to benefit most and which ones have the most difficulty learning within the current design and pedagogy. There are not universally good or bad programs or practices - only those that work or don't work for particular students given their prior education, background, interests, and abilities. This leads to assessments based on multiple measures and conducted at multiple points in time. For the adult student enrolling in the single course, it may mean assessment conducted solely within that course. For each and every diploma, certificate, and degree program the college offers, however, it also calls for (a) a clear articulation of learning goals, (b) learning activities specifically to attain those goals, (c) criteria for ascertaining learning achievement relative to those goals, (d) standards of performance for entry, progress, and graduation in the program, (e) assessment methods and measures that make sense relative to the goals, the students, and the institutional context, and (f) clear means for providing feedback from the assessment to students so they can improve their learning, to staff so that the programs and services can be improved and enhanced, and to the academic leadership, so the vision, priorities, planning, and direction of the institution can be charted. In this way, assessment can serve as both rudder and sail in bringing about effective program, staff, and organizational development.

References

Adelman, C. (1998). "A little night data on college student attendance patterns and course-taking:' paper presented at the annual forum of the Education Commission of the States, Portland, OR, July 7, 1998.

Astin, A.W. (1991). *Assessment for Excellence: The Philosophy and Practice of Assessment and Evaluation in Higher Education.* San Francisco: Jossey-Bass.

Barnett, R. (1992). *Improving Higher Education: Total Quality Care.* London: Society for Research in Higher Education and the Open University Press.

Bensimon, E. M. (1990). The new president and understanding the campus as a culture In W. G. Tierney (ed.), *Assessing Academic Climates and Cultures. New Directions for Institutional Research.* No. 68. San Francisco: Jossey-Bass.

Bolman, L. G., & Deal, T. E. (1991). *Reframing Organizations: Artistry, Choice, and leadership.* San Francisco: Jossey-Bass.

Clark, B. R. (1972). The organizational saga in higher *education. Administrative Science Quarterly,* 17, 179-194.

Farmer, D. (1999). "Course-Embedded Assessment: A Catalyst for Realizing the Paradigm Shift from Teaching to Learning." *Journal of Staff, Program, and Organizational Development,* 16(4): 35-47

Forsythe, G. B. and Keith, B. (1999). "Assessing Program Effectiveness: Design and Implementation of a Comprehensive Assessment Plan." *Journal of Staff, Program, and Organizational Development,* 16(4): 19-34

Furhmann, B.S. & Grasha, A.F. (1983). *College Teaching: A Practical Handbook.* Boston: Little, Brown & Co.

Jones, E.A. & Ratcliff, J.L. (1991). Which general education curriculum is better: Core curriculum or the distributional requirement, *Journal of General Education, 40* (1), 69-101.

Institute for Higher Education Policy. (1998). *College Remediation: What It Is, What It Costs, What's at Stake.* Washington, DC: author.

Keith, B. (1999). "The Institutional Context of Departmental Prestige in American Higher Education." *American Educational Research Journal.* 36(3): 409-445.

LaPotin, A. S. and Haessig, C. J. (1999). "Fostering Faculty Leadership in the Institutional Assessment Process." *Journal of Staff, Program, and Organizational Development,* 16(4) 49-56.

Lindquist, J. (1996). Strategies for change. In J. Gaff and J. L. Ratcliff (eds.), *Handbook of the Undergraduate Curriculum: A Comprehensive Guide to Purposes, Structures, Practices, and Change.* San Francisco: Jossey-Bass.

Marchese, T. (1987). Third down, ten years to go. *AAHE Bulletin, 40,* 3-8.

Montgomery, B. (1995). The relationship between higher education and society: A dialogic perspective on the autonomy / connection contra diction. Paper presented at the Annual Forum of the European Association for Institutional Research, Zurich, Switzerland, August 1995.

Morgan, G. (1986). *Images of Organization.* Newbury Park, CA: Sage, 1986.

Neave, G. & Van Vught, F. (1994). Government and higher education in developing nations: A conceptual framework. In G. Neave & F.

van Vught *(eds.). Government and Higher Education Relationships across Three Continents: The Winds of Change.* Tarrytown, NY-. Elsevier Science.

Shafer, R. J. (ed.). (1974). *A Guide to Historical Method.* Homewood, IL: Dorsey Press.

Ratcliff, J.L. & associates. (1995). *Realizing the Potential: Improving Postsecondary Teaching, Learning and assessment* University Park, PA: National Center on Postsecondary Teaching, Learning and Assessment, July 1995.

Reardon, M. F. & Ramaley, J. A. (1996). Building academic community while containing costs. In

Ratcliff, J. L. and Gaff, J. (eds.),(1996). *Handbook of the Undergraduate Curriculum: A Comprehensive Guide to Purposes, Structures, Practices, and Change.* San Francisco: Jossey-Bass.

Tierney, W. G. (1988). Organizational culture in higher education. *Journal of Higher Education,* 1988, 59(1), 2-21.

U.S. Department of Education, National Center for Education Statistics. (1996*a*). *Descriptive Summary of 1989-90 Beginning Postsecondary Students: 5 Year Later,* May 1996.

U.S. Department of Education, National Center for Education Statistics. (1996b). *The Condition of Education. Digest of Education Statistics.*

Van Vught, F. A. (1994). Intrinsic and extrinsic aspects of quality assessment in higher education. In D. F. Westerheijden, J. Brennan & P. A. M. Maassen (eds.), *Changing Contexts of Quality Assessment.* Utrecht: Lemma.

White, C.R. (1994). A model for comprehensive reform in general education. *Journal of General Education, 43* (3), 168-229.

Wright, B. D. (1996). Evaluating learning in individual courses. In J. Gaff and J. L. Ratcliff (eds.), *Handbook of the Undergraduate Curriculum: A Comprehensive Guide to Purposes, Structures, Practices, and Change.* San Francisco: Jossey-Bass.

James L. Ratcliff is formally professor and senior scientist at The Center for the Study of Higher Education, The Pennsylvania State University, University Park, PA.

Creating a Culture of Evidence: Learning Assessment at the Community College of Baltimore County

Henry F. Linck, Ed.D.
The Community College of Baltimore County

The current learning-centered reform in higher education is generally assumed to have gained impetus from the Wingspread Group on Higher Education report, *An American Imperative: Higher Expectations for Higher Education* published in 1993. In their seminal 1995 article on the learning paradigm, "From Teaching to Learning: A New Paradigm for Higher Education," Barr and Tagg declared the following:

A paradigm shift is taking hold in American Higher education. In its briefest form, the paradigm that has governed our colleges is this: A college is an institution that exists *to provide instruction.* Subtly but profoundly we are shifting to a new paradigm: A college is an institution that exists *to produce learning.* This shift changes everything. It is both needed and wanted. (p.13)

For the community college sector, the work of Terry O'Banion through the League for Innovation in the Community College became the driving force that embedded learning-centered language into the culture of the institution. In his book, *A Learning College for the 21st Century* (1997), O'Banion poses two central questions that are at the core of the learning college philosophy:

What does this student know?
What can this student do?

For O'Banion, "the learning college succeeds only when improved and expanded learning can be documented for its learners" (1997, p.60). The operative word here is, of course, *documented*. And as simple as it may seem, answers to these two questions along with the requisite documentation are difficult to obtain; but without clearly documented answers we cannot know that we are truly placing learning first. The Middle States Commission on Higher Education in its newly published *Characteristics of Excellence,* (2002, p. 50) includes "Assessment of Student Learning" as Standard 14:

> Assessment of student learning demonstrates that the institution's students have knowledge, skills, and competencies consistent with institutional goals and that students at graduation have achieved appropriate higher education goals.

The Commission further states, "In order to carry out meaningful assessment activities, institutions must articulate statements of expected student learning at the institutional, program, and individual course levels, although the level of specificity will be greater at the course level. Course syllabi or guidelines should include expected learning outcomes" (2002, p. 50). The remainder of this chapter will focus on one community college's response to this mandate and to the learning revolution in general.

The Community College of Baltimore County (CCBC)

The Community College of Baltimore County, Maryland, is a learning-centered public community college that anticipates and responds to the educational needs of the communities served by its three major campuses. It is the largest community college in Maryland with approximately 20,000 credit students enrolled each semester. Another 47,000 students attend classes annually through the Division of Continuing Education and Economic Development (CEED). About 56% of all Baltimore County residents who enroll in undergraduate education in Maryland attend CCBC. With 1,200 full-time employees, including 400 full-time faculty, 225 administrative and professional personnel, and 575 support staff, and an additional 800 adjunct faculty, CCBC has a major commitment to learning within its sphere of influence.

Using as its foundation the concept of the learning college as defined by O'Banion (1997) and Barr and Tagg (1995), Chancellor Irving Pressley McPhail created the *LearningFirst Strategic Plan* to guide the evolution of CCBC into a premier learning college of the 21st century. The philosophy driving the plan is embodied in the College's statement of beliefs: As a learning-centered community college, CCBC will do the following:

- Make learning its central focus.
- Make students active partners in the learning process.
- Assume final responsibility for producing student learning.
- Focus on learning outcomes to assess student learning and success.
- Create a holistic environment that supports student learning.

- Ensure that every member of the college community is a learner.
- Evaluate all areas of the college by the ways they foster student learning. (McPhail, 2001, p. 19)

The College's strategic plan established the vision of the College as a student-centered learning environment having as its core strategic direction, student learning. In addition, McPhail (1998) identified seven supporting strategic directions that make up the plan's framework: learning support, learning college, infusing technology, management excellence, embracing diversity, enrollment management, and building community.

- **Student Learning** establishes learning as the core value and direction of CCBC. All other actions are evaluated and judged on the basis of this proposition. CCBC's goal is to provide a high-quality, learning-centered education that maximizes student learning and makes students partners in their education. Students must be able to frame and achieve their educational goals and develop skills that are appropriate for the 21st. century.
- **Learning Support** provides a comprehensive and responsive support system that increases student access to learning opportunities and recognizes that the student is central to the learning process. CCBC's learning support goals are to increase student retention and success, create seamless instructional and student support services, improve student skills assessment and course placement, and increase community access to programs and services.
- The concept of the **Learning College** provides the impetus for CCBC's transformation into a learning college: that is, promoting the free exchange of ideas, encouraging innovation, emphasizing continuous improvement

through organizational learning, and focusing on assessment through a comprehensive institutional effectiveness and evaluation system.

- **Infusing Technology** recognizes and advances the use of new instructional technologies to enhance student learning as well as the general use of technology to improve the effectiveness and efficiency of college operations.

- **Management Excellence** facilitates the efficient and effective use of resources by linking planning and budgeting. This strategy promotes low-cost access to the college by ensuring efficient operations and focusing on generating additional resources.

- **Embracing Diversity** focuses on attracting and retaining a diverse faculty, staff, and student community. This goal is accomplished through initiatives that (a) advance a learning environment that encourages and values diversity, (b) incorporate diversity into the curriculum, and (c) recognize and address diverse learning styles.

- **Building Community** defines CCBC as an active member of the larger community. As such, CCBC takes a leading role in workforce training throughout the region and forms partnerships to support both local and regional economic and community development efforts.

- **Strategic Enrollment Management** (SEM) is designed to optimize enrollment in a manner that supports the development of a learning-centered college. This includes the creation of organizational structures, policies, procedures and information channels to support enrollment management as well as a continuous review of policies and practices that may inhibit the enrollment and retention of students. (McPhail, Heacock, Linck, 2001, pp. 20-21)

The *LearningFirst Strategic Plan* defines CCBC as a learning-centered institution and illustrates a clear commitment to making learning the institution's central focus, making students active partners in the learning process, and focusing on learning outcomes to assess the success of student learning. The focus on assessing learning outcomes is at the heart of the learning college philosophy and embodies the shift from teaching to learning.

Leading Change

The shift from teaching to learning is a major cultural change for most institutions and requires a planned and methodical implementation strategy. John Kotter's, *Leading Change* (1996) provides a concise framework for looking at the challenges of institutional transformation and strategies for implementing change.

The first two stages of Kotter's eight-stage process are relevant here. Kotter suggests that the first stage of the change process involves establishing a **sense of urgency** through examining the market and competitive realities and/or through identifying and discussing crises, potential crises or major opportunities. (1996, pp. 35-49) This principle is similar to O'Banion's concept of the "trigger event," the urgent event that gives organizational change its initial momentum. (1996, p.227) CCBC actually had two "trigger events": (1) the legislative mandate to merge three independent and autonomous community colleges into a single college and (2) the implementation of the *LearningFirst Strategic Plan*. Either one of these "events" might have been sufficient for an organization to declare a sense of urgency; the fact is, CCBC actually embarked upon two enormous transformations simultaneously, and each was dependent on the other for success. It is important to note that institutional transformation and change strategies are not necessarily linear. The transformation must be orchestrated so that all the myriad parts are in harmony; some parts may receive more emphasis at any given time, but they all continue to play at the same time. For CCBC, many of the tasks involved in merging three institutions were facilitated by the concurrent implementation of learning college perspectives.

Kotter's second stage of organizational change centers on creating a **guiding coalition** (1996, pp. 51-66). He points out that "individuals alone, no matter how competent or charismatic, never have all the assets needed to overcome tradition and inertia except in very small organizations" and that a guiding coalition is essential in orchestrating successful institutional change. Recognizing the need for a strong guiding coalition, the Chancellor of CCBC established the Council on Innovation and Student Learning (CISL), the single most important innovation contributing to the timely and effective implementation of *The LearningFirst Strategic Plan*.

The Council on Innovation and Student Learning (CISL)

At the beginning of the 1998-1999 academic year, the Chancellor established CISL to serve as the college-wide think tank to lead the transformation of CCBC into a premier, learning-centered college. The chancellor's charge to CISL was straightforward:

- Serve as a college-wide think tank.
- Lead the transformation of CCBC into a premier, learning-centered college.
- Serve as change agents
- Help to frame policies, procedures, and infrastructure needed to become a learning college
- Educate the institution and the campus communities.
- Develop a CCBC-specific operational definition of "learning".

- Stimulate the development of a college-wide process for experimentation and innovation.
- Document the change process and establish campus-based CISL organizations.

Membership in the Council on Innovation and Student Learning included faculty, professional non-teaching employees, students, and classified staff from each of the three campuses and from the Division of Continuing Education and Economic Development, and a representative from the Board of Trustees. The Vice Chancellor for Learning and Student Development and a faculty co-chairperson provide leadership for the group which has been responsible for developing a "new-faculty" learning community (a year long orientation program), for providing learning college staff development opportunities for all college employees, for developing teaching and learning centers on each campus, and for keeping the college community informed and educated about its efforts. The focus of CISL has changed each year to meet the College's changing needs and goals; but, over time, it was through CISL that *LearningFirst* became the voice of the College and not just the voice of the administration. This coalition continues to lead the *LearningFirst* agenda and is largely responsible for CCBC's successful transformation.

One of the major results of CISL's inaugural year's work was the development of a CCBC learning assessment plan by the learning outcomes assessment sub-committee: *The Guide for Learning Outcomes Assessment and Classroom Learning Assessment.* This guide defined the learning college for CCBC as an institution that "places learning first and provides educational experiences for learners anyway, anyplace, anytime" (O'Banion 1995-96, p. 22). Premised on the fundamental belief that learning outcomes assessment are a natural and ongoing component of the instructional process, the plan sought to provide faculty with a comprehensive and flexible process that would both encourage and stimulate learning outcomes assessment. However, from the beginning of the process of developing the plan, it was apparent that a number of issues would have to be addressed and eventually resolved. The issues were really very predictable, and are expressed in the following series of questions:

1. How is it possible to measure student learning?
2. Can we create an environment that encourages risk-taking and experimentation?
3. What if we find that we are not as good as we think we are? Will this affect overall institutional quality and morale?
4. Can we provide sufficient training so that everyone has the same understandings about the assessment process?
5. How do we provide sufficient institutional research and project design support for faculty who are not always well schooled in research design and implementation?
6. Will faculty be able to develop a common set of measurable course and program outcomes?
7. What will we do with the data once we collect it? How will we disseminate it?

Addressing the Issues

The first question usually asked about learning outcomes assessment is "How do you measure student learning?" Institutions have often responded by providing indirect measures of learning such as exit interviews with graduates, employer surveys to determine graduate preparedness, and at community colleges, transfer studies to track the success of students as they move on to four-year colleges and universities. Most institutions also employ other measures that purportedly assess student learning. These include student satisfaction surveys, program evaluation, local, state and other external reporting requirements, student grades, and retention rates. While all of these "measures" may say something about institutional effectiveness, they do not measure student learning in any direct way. Direct measures of learning require a different kind of assessment that is part of a long-term, dynamic process involving a multi-method approach. Standardized tests, portfolio assessments, capstone courses/experiences, pre and post-tests and externally reviewed and evaluated exhibitions and performances are among the more direct measures of student learning.

For an assessment plan to be effective it must be carried out in a risk-free environment. Faculty need to know that assessment results will not be used punitively against them or their students. The results should only be used to determine the best course of action for improving student learning. Building an environment of trust where faculty are free to experiment and test and change is an essential goal of any assessment system. And, in addition, providing training and related support for faculty and staff is important to resolve any misunderstandings about the purpose of assessment and to dispel any negative reactions to the idea of "measuring" learning.

It is equally important to address the issue of quality. Faculty invariably ask, "What if we find we're not as good as we think we are? Perhaps it's just better not to know!" Invariably, assessment results will indicate areas where improvement is needed, where changes to the curriculum are appropriate, and where learning can be improved. The more pressing question might be, "In an era of increasing accountability at all levels of higher education, can an institution afford not to know that it isn't as good as it thinks it is?" The real risk in not knowing is that nothing changes and learning neither improves nor expands.

Other issues include the difficulties associated with developing measurable course and program outcomes, in selecting good measures of those outcomes and in collecting and interpreting the data, and finally, the difficulties in disseminating assessment data and information. CCBC believes that building an assessment plan that incorporates these and a myriad of other concerns will, in part, assure its successful implementation.

CCBC's Learning Outcomes Assessment Program

CCBC's Learning Outcomes Assessment Program, implemented in 1999, supports the notion that evaluating the effectiveness of instruction is a faculty responsibility that is necessary for the improvement and verification of learning. As such, the process of assessing learning outcomes is a means to an end, that end being improved and expanded student learning. As part of the professional responsibility that goes with teaching, faculty identify, design, and implement specific learning assessment projects. The results, once analyzed, form the base for organized change that will have a positive influence on student learning. Learning outcomes assessment is neither precise nor perfect, and its data are interpreted with that in mind. It is a way of thinking about quality that comes from our willingness to continually examine, question, and, as necessary, alter what we do as an educational institution. This philosophy is consistent with traditional instructional practices.

CCBC implements this philosophy with a program of faculty-designed and institution-supported research projects. Faculty are empowered by the administration to develop an externally valid and reliable research design for assessing the learning outcomes of a particular course or program. In general, the process begins with the common course outline (see appendix A). In anticipation of the College's learning assessment plan, the faculty developed common course outlines for all courses; the outlines, not to exceed two pages in length, include ten to fifteen learning outcomes (measurable objectives) for which all instructors, both full-time and part-time, are minimally responsible. Faculty are encouraged to add additional course objectives, but those on the common course outline are required of all instructors. These measurable objectives provide the foundation for the assessment projects. Because the projects are faculty driven, faculty select the design of the research and the tools to measure the outcomes. And while they have many frameworks to choose from in the *Guide,* all projects must include some form of external validation on the premise that grades are an insufficient measure of student learning and that controlling for extraneous variables including instructor variability is essential.

The projects are a minimum of three semesters in length and include five stages:

1. Designing and proposing a learning outcomes assessment project;
2. Implementing the design and collecting and analyzing the data;
3. Redesigning the program/course to improve student learning;
4. Implementing program/course revisions and reassessing student learning;
5. Analyzing and reporting the results.

Course changes and reassessments can be implemented multiple times until faculty are satisfied that results yield improvement.

Stage one involves the faculty, either individually or in teams, working with the Learning Outcomes Associate (LOA), a faculty member who is an expert advisor who oversees the design process. The College LOA works with the faculty to develop the research design and to ensure that external validity and reliability are prioritized in choosing or developing the data collection tool. This type of research does not come naturally to all faculty, so the associate also provides staff development. Many faculty, particularly in the humanities and arts, have not taken coursework in research design and statistics. The Office of Institutional Research provides support for data analysis, especially for statistical procedures with which faculty may not be familiar.

Project proposals must address the operationalized objectives in the common course outline that are to be measured, an appropriate method for collecting data that measure the identified learning outcomes, some component of external validation, controls (all sections and instructors must implement the research in the same manner; sufficient sample size must be determined), data analysis, course improvement, reassessment after course revision, and dissemination of results. After the proposal is approved, faculty receive the first portion of an established stipend.

Stage 2 is the implementation phase with administration of the assessment instrument and the collection of relevant data. If the results indicate that subsequent stages are unnecessary, the faculty member or the assessment team prepares a final report for dissemination. If the results suggest a need for improvement, the project moves into stage 3, the redesign phase in which faculty design course improvements based on the data analysis. At this point faculty receive the second portion of the established stipend. Stage 4 involves the implementation of course revisions and a period of reassessment using the same instrument as in Stage 2. Data is collected and analyzed by comparing the results of this stage with the results identified in Stage 2. Stage 5 is the final reporting phase with results disseminated to campus libraries and other relevant faculty. The final stipend payment is made at the conclusion of this final stage of the project.

It is important to reiterate that this research must be done in **a risk-free environment.** The purpose of any outcomes assessment process is to improve student learning, not to punish faculty or students if results are less than optimal. The major role of the administration is to encourage and support faculty as they undertake these projects. The compensation is not connected with the results but rather with the process.

The Evolution of CCBC's Learning Assessment Plan

CCBC's Learning Assessment Plan has evolved through three distinct phases: individual course assessment, high impact/high enrollment course assessment, and program assessment. Initially, the plan began with individual course assessment where individual faculty members volunteered to assess learning in one of their courses. In this "volunteer stage" faculty were encouraged to respond to a request for proposals to develop a learning outcomes assessment project for one of their courses. The first RFP resulted in eighteen projects, most of which were submitted by individual faculty members; however, several faculty members from a single discipline submitted joint proposals. The same process was implemented in the following year, with an equal number of faculty submitting proposals; eighteen new projects were approved for a total of 36 projects at various stages of the process in the second year. It was evident that the learning assessment process at CCBC was quickly becoming institutionalized. Admittedly, these projects, because they were course and instructor specific, affected the learning of a relatively low number of students; something less than 700 students would be directly affected by the curricular changes implemented as a result of the findings in these initial projects.

First Round Projects

A chemistry department chair submitted a proposal in the first round of projects that would assess students' skills in the laboratory portion of an Introduction to Chemistry course. As a result of the first assessment, changes were made in how skills were taught and how the skills were assessed. Now in the third phase of the project, the project leader reported that two new lab experiments were developed and incorporated into the lab program. These new exercises were developed to provide skills that were identified during the early phases of the project as needed for students exiting the program but were still not included in the existing curriculum.

In Phase III, students were assessed at midterm and at the end of the semester. Assessments were conducted using the assessment instruments (18 skills measures) developed in Phase II of the project. Assessment results were analyzed

Table 1: CHEM 108 Strong Performance Areas

Skill Area	% Students scoring 3.0 or above
Light lab burner	93.4%
Increase burner flame	94.7%
Decrease burner flame	84.2%
Weigh directly on electronic balance	85.5%
Weigh by difference	80.3%
Measure volume with graduated cylinder	89.5%
Test pH with litmus paper	98.7%
Proper disposal of waster material	80.0%
Measure volume with pipet	81.6%
Measure absorbance with colorimeter	84.3%

*Scores on a five point scale: Outstanding=5, Satisfactory=3-4, Needs Improvement=2, Unsatisfactory=1

for individual students, class sections, and for all students as a group. The key results are as follows:

- Using an average overall score of 3.0 or higher as a criterion, the majority (89.5%) of CHEM 108 students performed at the satisfactory level or better overall for the 17 skills categories assessed.

- The data for all students reveal strong performance in the following areas (percentages represent students scoring 3.0 or higher in a particular skill (see Table 1).

- The following data (Table 2) represent skills assessed as weak in terms of student performance (students scored less than three).

Analyses of these results lead to the formulation of a number of recommendations:

- Greater emphasis must be placed on basic laboratory techniques with less emphasis on information that can be delivered through the lecture portion of the course.

Table 2: CHEM 108 Weak Performance Skills Identified

Skill Area	% Students scoring less than 3.0
Measure length with a ruler	39.5%
Measure volume with a buret	48.6%
Adherence to safety regulations	27.6%
Prepare a solution of accurate concentration with a volumetric flask	38.6%
Measure temperature accurately with a thermometer	25.7%

*Scores on a five point scale: Outstanding=5, Satisfactory=3-4, Needs Improvement=2, Unsatisfactory=1

- A new laboratory text has been identified that is focused more on techniques than information content. The existing lab manual was developed several years ago by the faculty but lacks a student-learning focus and would require much revision to become "learner friendly". It was recommended, therefore, that a new laboratory text be adopted. (As a follow-up activity, the project leader subsequently authored a learner-centered laboratory manual through the College's summer grants program that provides support for faculty to develop learner-centered innovations).

- Skills assessment should be a mandatory and permanent part of the lab program, and direct observation of students performing lab skills, rather than written exams, should be the primary assessment technique.

This particular project is a good example the continuous quality improvement that can occur as a result of a learning outcomes assessment project.

Interestingly enough, the initial projects reflected a broad range of design. For example, a CADD (computer-aided design and drafting) professor utilized portfolio assessment to measure his students' outcomes, using a subset of the National Occupational Skills Standards for CADD to measure the outcomes. The goal of this project was to assess the learning outcomes in a two semester CADD Engineering Drawing course to determine if CADD students were achieving at levels necessary to become productive employees at local engineering, design and architectural companies. At the completion of CADD 241, a capstone course, students submitted a portfolio of their work to be evaluated in terms of industry skills standards developed by the U.S. Department of Education. A subset of these skills was selected and presented to industry professionals and a sample set of student portfolios was used to "norm" the products. Student portfolios were forwarded to an industry professional for examination. The following suggestions were made by the industry professional to the CADD program coordinator:

- Continue and increase the use of metric drawings including dual dimensioning;
- Incorporate inclusion of "real world" experiences;
- Introduce the concepts relating to the "process of drawing" to include beginning of design and engineering changes, release of drawing for production and archiving;
- Create an example where the student will use the Web to acquire information or product data;
- Explore ways to infuse a collaborative experience into the learning environment.

Based on these recommendations, this professor implemented the following changes to the curriculum:

1. Approximately 25% of the lab work assigned now involves the use of the metric system.
2. "Real-world" experiences encountered on the job as a mechanical engineer are introduced to the class using drawings and designs produced by the instructor who is an industry professional.
3. In addition to the use of the text chapter on "the process of drawing," the instructor emphasizes this topic by assessing student drawings and giving students the opportunity to resubmit their drawings after correction. This is consistent with industry practice.
4. The students now conduct a web search for a drawing which they are required to dimension and annotate.
5. At this time, collaboration is limited to students' assisting each other when faced with a drawing or design problem. In the subsequent course, a final project will require the incorporation of a collaborative experience.

This project will be repeated to determine if the curricular changes that were implemented based upon the pre-test assessment are positively impacting student learning.

In another project, two psychology professors administered the CLEP test, a nationally normed standardized test, as the final examination in the course, Introduction to Psychology, along with a departmentally developed final exam in a post-test only design. All of the students earning A's or B's, 60% of students earning C's, and 36% of students earning D's on the internal evaluation instrument passed the CLEP. Therefore, findings showed that the departmental final exam grades correlated with the standardized CLEP grades (r=.70). The professors also discovered no differences in student achievement by most demographic variables or by course section.

Another faculty member used an external grader to assess her students' learning outcomes by inviting a professor at another college to evaluate speeches in an Introduction to Speech class. Two English professors used outside consultants to assess student essays while providing lists of expected outcomes and a grading rubric to the consultant. Other faculty used pre- and post-testing as a basic research design. This was especially helpful in disciplines where an external test was not easily available.

Second Round Projects

In the second year of the assessment plan, a Learning Outcomes Assessment Advisory Board was established to provide broad-based support for learning assessment and to recommend policy and procedural changes as the implementation of the plan continued. This widely representative group suggested a change in how the projects were determined in order to improve and expand learning for a larger number of students. The advisory board suggested moving from the "volunteer stage" of individual faculty involved in single course/

section assessment to a "high impact/high enrollment" course implementation that would be mandatory for all faculty involved in teaching any one of the high impact courses selected. The most remarkable aspect here is that this change was universally accepted as a natural next step in the process. For CCBC this was clear evidence that learning assessment had become institutionalized. And, most importantly, an environment of trust had been established where faculty felt free to experiment, to take risks, and to engage in learning assessment without the fear of punitive measures for whatever the assessments might reveal.

The first five "high impact/high enrollment" learning outcomes assessment projects involved upper level developmental courses in reading, mathematics and writing in addition to *Introduction to Accounting* and *Introduction to Psychology*. The projects for these high impact courses involved all faculty (full-time and part-time) on all three campuses teaching these specific courses. A faculty member in the discipline who was assisted by a core of faculty to develop and implement the project headed each project. These projects had the potential of affecting the learning of as many as 7,000 students, far more than the 700 in the first two years of the program.

Third Round High Impact Projects

The high impact reading project, Developmental Reading (RDNG 052), is one of three high enrollment developmental projects, in addition to developmental writing and mathematics. The reading departments administered the nationally-normed Nelson-Denny reading test to all CCBC students enrolled in RDNG 052 (Level II Reading) at the beginning of the course (Pre-test Form G) and at the completion of the course (Post-test Form H). The test measures both literal and inferential reading skills and is normed at the community college level. This study attempted to identify gains in reading comprehension in general and to identify the number of students actually reading at college level by the end of the course. To provide an incentive for students to do well on the test, students were told that if they scored high enough, they would be waived from the RDNG 052 requirement. They were given the standard time to take the tests.

Additionally, all RDNG 052 students were given the Learning and Study Strategies Inventory (LASSI), pre- and post-test, in order to identify self-perception of study behaviors and positive attitudes that lead to success in college (noncognitive variables for success). These behaviors and attitudes, expected upon a student's completion of the developmental program, include the following:

- Makes informed choices by thinking critically.
- Accepts responsibility for educational progress and his/her role in the process.
- Demonstrates an understanding of who he/she is as a learner and a knowledge of learning techniques that are personally effective.
- Accepts and accesses resources as necessary.
- Demonstrates an ability to construct knowledge.
- Is able to learn from other students.
- Exhibits confidence as a learner.
- Appreciates diverse perspectives and recognizes the added value of these perspectives.

Only students who had completed the course and who had completed both pre and post tests were included in the sample. Forty-five percent of the fall 2001 RDNG 052 students (409) at CCBC comprised the sample. Of the sample, approximately half were white, 40% were African-American, and 10% were of other ethnicities. Sixty-eight percent were age 19 or younger, 17% were between the ages of 20 and 24, and 15% were older than 24. Sixty-five percent were female.

An analysis of the Nelson-Denny Reading Test scores using matched pairs analysis shows that on average CCBC students moved from the 19th to the 27th percentile on the national, community college norms as a result of taking the course. The changes in the mean scores pre- and post-test are presented in Table 3. A matched-pairs sample t-test resulted in statistically significant mean differences between pre- and post-test scores (mean difference=3.5) overall (t =12.76, df = 408, Sig.= 0.00). The data indicate that the majority of students (74%) scored higher on the post-test than on the pre-test. The range, depending upon the campus, was from 62 % to 84%.

Differences were further analyzed by comparing interpretive (inferential) scores to literal scores. Although students showed little to no change in their literal scores, they scored significantly higher on the interpretive questions on all three campuses (Table 4). Because the focus of the course is on critical reading rather than on literal reading, as described in the common course outline, the larger gain in interpretation was appropriate and encouraging.

Table 3: Paired Samples T Test of Nelson-Denny Test Results

	Paired Differences (Pre-Post)					t	df	Sig. (2-tailed)
	Mean Difference	Std. Deviation	Std. Error Mean	95% Confidence Interval of the Difference				
				Lower	Upper			
Total Score Pre/post difference	3.5	5.50	0.27	2.93	4.00	12.76	408	0.00

The results of the administration of the LASSI to address non-cognitive variables that may affect student success in RNDG 052 are presented in Tables 5 and 6. Students showed considerable growth on 10 out of 12 of the LASSI scales and statistically significant differences between their pretest scores and posttest scores on 11 out of 12 scales. Scales in which students showed the most growth included anxiety, concentration, information processing, selecting main idea, study aids, self-testing, and test strategies. In all of these scales, students moved up on their percentile ranking by approximately 15 to 20 points. Percentiles were derived from the scores of community college students across the country.

The learning outcomes assessment project for RDNG 052 showed that most students improve their reading skills by the time they complete RDNG 052. Although gains did not indicate that students had college-level reading skills by the end of the course, most students had experienced at least six months' growth in reading skills. As a "rule of thumb," most reading experts expect that at least 60 hours of instruction are needed for a learner to achieve a full year's growth in reading skills. In this case, students had approximately 45 hours of instruction; therefore, the fact that they did not move

Table 4: Paired Samples Test of Nelson-Denny Test Results

	Paired Differences (Pre-Post)					t	df	Sig. (2-tailed)
	Mean Difference	Std. Deviation	Std. Error Mean	95% Confidence Interval of the Difference				
				Lower	Upper			
Literal	0.2	3.20	0.16	-0.08	0.54	1.45	408	0.15
Interpretive	3.2	3.28	0.16	2.90	3.60	19.93	408	0.00

up to college level is not surprising. Another factor was the low level at which students began the RDNG 052 course. This factor is the basis of the first recommendation: that the cut-score on the ETS Accuplacer between RDNG 051 and 052 be re-examined. Widespread differences in gains on the Nelson-Denny among the campuses suggested that instructional practices should be examined to determine possible factors for success. In particular, one campus experienced gains that were more than twice as great as those of the other two campuses, despite the fact that the pre-test scores were lower than those on the other two campuses. Especially encouraging were the large gains made by African-American students, who entered with lower than average pre-test scores. This campus uses an approach for its required lab that differs from the approach at the other two campuses. This approach, researched in the pilot, uses a direct application of reading skills with articles found on the Internet. Thus a second recommendation from this learning assessment project is that the other two cam-

Table 5: Summary Percentiles of CCBC LASSI Results

	CCBC Mean Pre-Test Score	Normed Percentile	CCBC Mean Post Test Score	Normed Percentile
Attitude	33.6	71	34.4	71
Motivation	32.4	60	32.8	60
Time Management	26.6	73	28.2	76
Anxiety	24.2	38	27.2	55
Concentration	27.6	68	30	81
Information Processing	26.6	53	28.7	68
Selecting Main Idea	18	53	19.8	78
Study Aids	23.7	47	26	63
Self Testing	26.8	66	28.6	79
Test Strategies	28.6	45	30.8	62

puses pilot a few sections with this approach to see if it might yield the same results.

A third finding of this learning outcomes assessment project concerns the lack of growth in literal comprehension. Although, as stated earlier, the course primarily focuses on critical reading skills, students need to be continuing to grow in their ability to literally comprehend texts. Literal comprehension is very dependent on vocabulary skills and paraphrasing skills. A third recommendation from this project was to redirect more instructional time toward paraphrasing and summarizing difficult texts.

Program Assessment

The final stage in the evolution of CCBC's assessment plan focused on program assessment. While the college has a regular process for evaluating career and transfer programs on a five-year cycle, a new requirement calls for a program level learning outcomes assessment project as one part of the total program evaluation process. This requirement became effective in the Fiscal Year 2003 program evaluation year.

Table 6: Number of Cases where Post Test Score was Greater than Pre-test Score on LASSI

		N	%
ATT	Attitude	136	52%
MOT	Motivation	127	49%
TMT	Time Management	148	57%
ANX	Anxiety	170	65%
CON	Concentration	170	65%
INP	Information Processing	157	60%
SMI	Selecting Main Idea	167	64%
STA	Study Aids	167	64%
SFT	Self Testing	151	58%
TST	Test Strategies	166	64%

In addition to changing the program review process, the College also developed a new General Education Program for implementation in the Fall of 2001. The General Education Review Board, recognizing the need for assessing general education program goals, spent more than one year gathering assessment information from community colleges in Maryland and across the country to identify best practices in the area of General Education assessment. As a result of the research, the General Education Review Board designed a multi-dimensional assessment plan to include feedback from three primary sources: The ETS Student Instructional Report II (SIR II); the Academic Profile; and common graded assignments (CGAs) in specific discipline areas. The latter became known as the GREAT (GeneRal Education Assessment Team) Project.

The SIR II, a standardized course evaluation instrument used by all faculty at CCBC, allows the institution to include up to ten specifically designed questions that can be added to the standard 46-question questionnaire. For the first time in the Fall of 2002, students responded to four specifically designed questions concerning their General Education program goals.

In addition, the Academic Profile, a standardized test of general knowledge, was administered to a large sample of students in the Fall of 2001; these results serve as benchmarks for comparing future results. The Academic Profile was administered in Speech 101, a course that all degree seeking students must take but not necessarily early in their academic careers at the college. Consequently, responses can be sorted by the number of credits accumulated so that "value added" could be determined comparing results from students early and late in their coursework. CCBC plans to administer the Academic Profile at least once every three years to monitor student performance in relationship to the general education program goals.

The GREAT Project

The third source of feedback involves the General Education Assessment Team (GREAT) project. The purpose of the GREAT Project is to design and administer Common Graded Assignments (CGAs), and to develop accompanying scoring rubrics designed by faculty teams to assess the first six General Education Program goals. These goals are as follows (The phrases in bold that follow each goal are the abbreviated terms that are included in the common graded assignment rubric form—see Appendix B.):

1. Introduce students to the fundamental principles, concepts, vocabulary, and methods essential for the acquisition of knowledge and skills basic to the field of study; **(Content, Knowledge, and/or Skills)**
2. Prepare students to communicate effectively using written and oral or signed communication skills; **(Written, Oral and/or Signed Communication Skills)**
3. Provide a variety of learning experiences that encourage students, independently and in collaboration with others, to use those fundamental principles and methods to acquire, analyze, and use information for purposes of inquiry, critical thinking, problem-solving, and creative expression in a diverse environment; **(Critical Thinking Skills)**
4. Prepare students to adapt to change, including the increasing integration of information technology in all fields of knowledge and expression; **(Technology as a Learning Tool)**
5. Provide students with the knowledge and skills to understand themselves and others from various cultural, social, aesthetic, political, and environmental perspectives; **(Cultural Appreciation)** and
6. Provide the experiences that will allow students to become independent learners, the skills to analyze their

strengths and weaknesses as learners, and the knowledge to accomplish the tasks involved in learning. **(Independent Learning Skills)**

The GREAT Project is a faculty driven initiative. Early in the Fall 2001 semester, a subcommittee of the Learning Outcomes Assessment Advisory Board, working in conjunction with the General Education Review Board, designed a comprehensive training program and invited faculty to attend to learn how to design common graded assignments and scoring rubrics for each General Education Program discipline. With over 60 faculty members attending, each discipline formed a team, and one faculty member from each team served as team leader for the following General education categories as mandated by the Maryland Higher Education Commission: Arts and Humanities, Social Sciences, Diversity, Mathematics, Biological and Physical Sciences, Information Literacy/Technology, Wellness and Health, and Global, Historical, and Cultural Perspectives. The goal for the first pilot was to include one course for each General Education category.

Course	Title	General Education Category
CINS 101	Introduction to Computers	Information Literacy/Technology
HLTH 101	Health and Wellness	Wellness and Health
SOCL 141	Racial and Cultural Minorities	Social Sciences/Diversity
SPCM 101	Fundamentals of Speech Communication	Arts and Humanities/Communication
PSYC 101	Introduction to Psychology	Social and Behavioral Sciences
RECR 242	Women and Leisure	Global, Historical, and Cultural Perspectives

Faculty teams were charged with designing one to three common graded assignments and accompanying scoring rubrics for their disciplines. Teams met over the course of three months to complete this work and had student assignments ready for the Spring 2002 pilot. This work culminated in common graded assignments for six courses:

Students submit two copies of the assignment: one with the student's name to be graded as part of the course requirements and one "blind" copy to be graded against the general education rubric by trained scorers after the course was completed. A half-day training workshop was provided to train faculty and staff who were interested in scoring the GREAT projects. The training was provided by an external consultant to assure reliability in scoring the projects. See Appendix B for an example of a common graded assignment designed for Introduction to Computers (CINS101) and Appendix C for the grading rubric prepared for assessing students' competencies. A pilot project was conducted for all six of the courses in the Spring of 2002 and yielded the following results.

Results cannot be compared from one course to another for a number of reasons, including the fact that the rubrics were very different from course to course, and the program goals were interpreted in different ways for different courses. One advantage of the GREAT Project is the amount of flexibility that faculty have to design the common graded assignments and rubrics to meet the needs of the learners in their specific courses; however, that may continue to limit the tabulation and interpretation of results across courses and disciplines. The data that has been gathered to date indicates that student learning related to the General Education Program goals is "average." As shown in Table 8, CCBC students score within the national norms on all of the subscores and the total score on the *Academic Profile* and preliminary results from the GREAT project also suggest that students' scores are in the average range (a score of 3.0 to 4.0 on a scale of 1-6.)

Institutionalizing Outcomes Assessment

For a learning outcomes assessment program to gain wide acceptance among faculty with the desired resulting cultural change, it needs to be showcased. At CCBC the Council on Innovation and Student Learning continues to play an important role in this effort. The Associate for Learning Outcomes Assessment and the Learning Outcomes Assessment Advisory Board continue to oversee and provide support at the college level for all projects. The Advisory Board has expanded its role to include further development and revision of the college-wide effort to institutionalize learning outcomes assessment at all levels.

Table 8: Average Category Scores of Common Graded Assignments

Rubric Category	CINS 101 N=15	HLTH 101 N=20	SOCL 141 N=15	SPCM 101 N=22	PSYC 101 N=9
Content	3.73	3.85	4.20	N/A	5.67
Communication	3.00	3.56	4.00	4.23	4.89
Critical Thinking	3.27	4.20	3.87	4.63	N/A
Technology	3.40	*2.00	N/A	3.38	5.33
Cultural Appreciation	3.63	*1.40	4.17	N/A	N/A
Independent Learning	3.23	4.18	3.77	N/A	N/A

* Students were expected to include a reference list as a part of the HLTH 101 CGA. The rubric suggested a score of 1 (as opposed to 0) for the following: *Uses no outside technological resources to develop and support the content and conclusion.*

Perhaps the most important activity that moved the outcomes assessment initiative beyond a few faculty volunteers and a committee is the Council on Innovation and Student Learning Fair that is held at least twice each academic year. In its first year, the council developed and implemented college-wide staff development programs used learning outcomes as the theme for one fair early in the process. A nationally recognized expert was brought in as the keynote speaker. The volunteer faculty had the opportunity to attend a variety of breakout sessions in which to discuss all phases of their projects: some focused on getting started, some on data collection, some on analysis and program revision. After this initial CISL fair focusing on learning outcomes, every subsequent CISL fair has offered breakout sessions featuring learning outcomes assessment projects provided by faculty for faculty. Similar presentations have been provided on each campus and at least one division ran its own version of a CISL fair so that colleagues were sharing within their disciplines and across closely related disciplines. Because of this continued presence of learning outcomes assessment in a strong staff development program, "learning outcomes assessment" is now part of the vocabulary of the institution, a given in our functioning.

The Board of Trustees is part of the dissemination effort as well. Each Board meeting includes *LearningFirst* presentations, and learning outcomes research projects have figured prominently in those presentations. Our local funding authority, a normally fiscally conservative group, has funded this project well. We successfully argued that we wanted to expand what had been our normal operation to institute a program to collect evidence that we were succeeding in our mission. The cost of the program is integrated into the operating budget and fully supported by CCBC's local funding authority.

Learning Outcomes Assessment "Successes"

CCBC has faced several challenges through its implementation of the Learning Outcomes Assessment Program, but at the same time has faced these challenges with many successes. As a result of the great strides CCBC has made in assessing both general education, as well as course and program outcomes, the institution has received national recognition as an outcomes assessment leader. CCBC continues to share its successes at multiple national conferences as one of 12 Vanguard learning colleges in the nation. Some of the successes in assessment include the following:

- Creating a "culture of assessment" with increased faculty participation and buy-in;
- Using outcomes assessment in program review;
- Forging new partnerships between faculty teams, institutional research staff, the Vice Chancellor's Office, and the outcomes associate in analyzing data and making curricular and pedagogical recommendations for change;
- Creating a newly updated *Guide for Learning Outcomes Assessment and Classroom Learning Assessment,* a model guide for assessment;
- Establishing the Learning Outcomes Assessment Advisory Board that provides leadership in credit and non-credit course/program assessment.

The projects continue to illustrate success through collaborative efforts among faculty teams who are enthusiastic about improving student learning and student success.

Summary and Next Steps

Learning outcomes assessment projects succeed only when the institution makes a commitment to them as integral to the College's mission. The faculty are then encouraged and empowered by the administration to see that this as a useful way to advance learning and to answer the question, "How do we know that learning has occurred?" For these projects to lead to institution-wide improvement of learning, they need to be grounded in common learning objectives developed by the faculty. Because it is at the faculty level that learning activities are based, the faculty are the primary instruments by which learning is facilitated. Consequently, it is only by empowering the faculty to gather data and implement strategics for improvement that this program can succeed. The administration's role is to provide the substantial assistance in the development of learning outcomes assessment and in the revision of instructional practices that follow from that assessment. Finally, sharing results and developing a climate of striving for improvement bring about institutionalization of this effort.

At CCBC, the next step will be to institutionalize learning outcomes assessments further by tying them into existing structures and by focusing on the wide range of services available to students to enhance student learning. It is fair to say that CCBC, as a premier learning college of the 21st century, is an outcomes driven institution which has established a culture of evidence that demonstrates that it has, indeed, improved and expanded student learning.

APPENDICES

Appendix A: Common Course Outline Checklist

Course Designator and Number_____

Course Title:_____ Reviewer:_____

Course Proposer: _____ Date:_____

_____

    Campus/Division/Phone no.

____ Approved without revisions   ____Resubmit with revisions

Approved Banner Form (course description, pre- and co- requisites, credits, etc.)

I.   Overall Course Objectives
      This section will:

____   a. focus on what students are able to do at the conclusion of the course;

____   b. include an introductory statement that reads: "Upon successful completion of this course, students will be able to:";

____   c. include approximately 10-15 measurable objectives (for 3-credit courses);

____   d. include objectives that begin with a verb appropriate to the learning domain

____   e. (cognitive, psychomotor, affective);

____   f. include verbs that measure higher level competencies as well as basic competencies;

____   g. include objectives that directly correlate to course requirements.

Comments:_____

_____

II.   Major Topics
      This section will:

____   a. list major content areas that are applicable to every section of the course that is offered;

____   b. reflect content that is critical for successful completion of the overall course objectives and course requirements.

Comments:_____

_____

III.   Course Requirements

This section will:

a.   include the introductory statement: "Specific assignments and procedures for evaluating student performance in this course will be described in the individual class syllabus. However, all students will:";

b.   include a minimum of two different assessment modes (e.g., exams, papers, oral presentations, labs, project);

c.   demonstrate that the course provides students with ongoing assessment of and communication about their learning progress;

d.   directly correlate with overall course objectives;

e.   quantitatively identify all minimum expectations for students (e.g., a minimum of three written examinations, two essays of 500-750 words, at least one group project).

Comments:_____

_____

Gen. Ed. Criteria	6	5	4	3	2	1
Content Knowledge and/or skills	Consistently exceeds stated requirements by interweaving and correlating multiple sets of facts; and presents them in a sophisticated manner using all three software packages.	Completes all stated requirements utilizing advanced features in three software packages. Material is neatly presented.	Finds eight–ten facts. Material is organized and presented using some advanced features of two software packages.	Finds six - seven facts and material is not clearly presented. Implies beginner's knowledge of one software package.	Finds three -- five facts and material presented is poorly organized. Uses minimal features of one software package.	Finds one – two facts and material presented is confusing and messy. Displays rudimentary knowledge of one software package.
Written, Oral, and/or Signed Communication Skills	Coherent and logically written. Excellent usage of vocabulary. No spelling or grammatical errors.	Clearly written. Excellent usage of vocabulary. Few spelling or grammatical errors.	Well written. Good usage of vocabulary. Some spelling / grammatical errors.	Moderate usage of vocabulary. Several spelling / grammatical errors.	Weak usage of vocabulary. Many spelling and grammatical errors.	Poorly written. Poor use of vocabulary. Too many spelling and grammatical errors.
Critical Thinking Skills	Exceptional choice of resources. Cites resources and comments on the reliability of the resources; develops comprehensive list of facts and correlates facts among and between resources; conveys facts in well organized groups supporting conclusions or editorial statements. Points out discrepancies in facts from different sources and uses these discrepancies to amplify or draw conclusion	Uses more than required resources and presents more than required facts. Choice of resources shows good judgment in selecting best source for statistic or content. Information is clearly target for a specific audience (business or recreational).	Uses all required resources and present all required facts. Content shows a developed picture of the country.	Uses almost all required resources 4 and finds almost all required facts 9-10. Facts presented show an understanding of some aspects of the country.	Fails to use the required number of resources and finds somewhat less then the required number of facts. Unable to find 2 required facts. Paper merely restates facts and does not present them in an interesting manner.	Fails to use the required number of resources. Writing does not use facts to present a substantial description. Unable to find 3 required facts.
Technology as a Learning Tool	Has mastery of major search engines, performs advanced Boolean searches to meet requirements; able to	Has greater depth of knowledge of specialty sites to specifically answer detailed information about a	Able to competently use the Internet to locate important information. Finds independent sources	Able to find and reference any of the search sites listed in the project outline. Can correlate info	Shows weakness or unfamiliarity with using the Internet when conducting research. Understands that there	Shows lack of skill with using the Internet when conducting research unable to find any facts that are not

Appendix B--Instructional Rubric for Assessing General Education Goals in CINS 101 (Continued)

Gen. Ed. Criteria	6	5	4	3	2	1
Technology as a Learning Tool (Continued)	identify multiple specialty information sources and refer to printed matter as well as internet sources; able to identify and utilize government, commercial and editorial sites for information gather and accurately identifies source in an appropriate manner. Consistently exceeds assignment requirements.	location; uses all sites referred to and at least as many sites independently identified to correlate data; able to find information presented in different ways (chart, text, tabular, etc, and sites each source individually	beyond those mentioned. Has knowledge of more than one specialty search site (mySimon, google, ask.Jeeves etc.)	between 2 sites. Able to find some answers to specific questions using search engines	is more than one way to find data on search engines and that specialty engines exist. Shows some facility for running more than one task	plainly visible. Unable to refer independently to more than the listed sites. Has difficulty culling data and information in one window and using the authoring software in another.
Cultural Appreciation	Superb appreciation and understanding of country demonstrated by end product.	Very good appreciation and understanding of country demonstrated by end product.	Shows appreciation and understanding of country demonstrated by end product.	Shows some appreciation and understanding of country demonstrated by end product.	Shows little appreciation and understanding of country demonstrated by end product.	Shows no appreciation of country demonstrated by end product.
Independent Learning Skills	Independently uses technology and research tools available. Consistently demonstrates creativity and the ability to independently learn new advanced features in all three software packages. Also brings personal experience with additional tools to bear in an appropriate manner	Makes excellent use of on-line resources and help tools to fully exploit features and function of multiple programs required for the presentations; confidently presents information from multiple sources in easy to understand format; prepares citations to substantiate all statements; Requires little or no guidance to perform tasks	Understands fully the tools available and their use; appropriately uses the software for appropriate function; integrates information independently and finds new sources of data to support ideas or other facts	Understands the required technology and has a general understanding as to the capabilities of the technology but is unsure how/where to look for help; performs the minimum required effort achieve passing grade	Works mostly independently, but requires additional assistance; seeks reinforcement that materials are appropriate; does not present a cogent approach to the project tasks.	Unable to use the Internet as a research tool and unable to apply acquired software skills. Requires much instructor assistance in carrying out research

Contexts for Learning

Appendix C: CINS Web Research Project

Scenario:

You have just landed your first professional job after graduating from CCBC at a local travel agency called ABROAD. As one of your job duties, you are hired to design some literature for prospective customers. You were hired because of the technical skills you possess in MS office and in your ability to locate information on the Web.

Assignment:

Part 1: Pick a country to research. Only one country per student per class, so sign up quickly.

Part 2: You are to use the Internet to gather information about your chosen country. You should use at least five resources (page 2). Include at least ten facts; the first three are required, from the list below.

• Current event	• Government Type
• Interesting Web Sites	• Economy
• Use of Technology	• Life Expectancy
• Location and map	• Tourism
• Size	• Food
• Population	• Religion
• Climate	• Dress
• Holidays	• Primary Languages
• Sports	Spoken
• Terrain	• Music
• Literacy	• Capital
• Unemployment rate	• Flag
• Industries	• Currency
• Military Branches	• Communication
	• Transportation

Part 3:
CINS101 – To complete this project, you will demonstrate software skills using a combination of Word, Excel, and PowerPoint. Examples are: a combination of a brochure, pamphlet, newsletter, chart, attractive table, at least 6 slides with animations and templates to show prospective customers. Be creative and original.

CINS155 – students will create a web page (non-published) or a PowerPoint presentation including at least 6 slides with animations and templates to show prospective customers.

Internet Information Resource

1. CCBC's Online Card Catalog
    o www.ccbcmd.edu
    o Library and other resources
    o CCBC Catonsville / Library
    o MILLIE (CCBC's Card Catalog)

2. Online Newspaper Databases
    o www.ccbcmd.edu
    o Library and other resources
    o CCBC Catonsville / Library
    o Electronic Resources
    o Scroll Down and Select Newspapers Online

3. Online Encyclopedia
    o www.ccbcmd.edu
    o Library and other resources
    o CCBC Catonsville / Library
       • Electronic Resources
       • Britannica Online

4. National or International News Website(ex. MSNBC, CNN....)
    o www.msnbc.com
    o www.cnn.com
    o www.usnews.com

5. Internet Search Engine or Web Subject Directories
    - www.ccbcmd.edu
        o   Library and other resources
        o   CCBC Catonsville / Library
        o   Internet Search Engines
        o   *Select a Search Engine*
    - www.ccbcmd.edu
        o   Library and other resources
        o   CCBC Catonsville / Library
        o   Web Subject Directories
        o   *Select a Subject Guide*

6. U.S. Census Bureau - International Programs Center
    - U.S.
        o   www.census.gov
    - World (International Database)
        o   www.census.gov
        o   From the People Category, select International
            (International Programs Center - IPC)
        o   International Database – IDB

7. CIA World Fact book from the C. I. A.
        o   www.odci.gov/cia/publications/factbook/index.html

8. Country Studies Department of the Army Country Studies/Area
    Handbook Program.
        o   lcweb2.loc.gov/frd/cs/cshome.html

9. Culture
        o   www.worldskip.com/

10. Portal to the World
        o   www.loc.gov/rr/international/portals.html

11. Yahoo
        o   www.yahoo.com
        o   Under Regional, Countries

Part 4: List the websites you used. This will serve as your references. What websites didn't you use from the Internet Information Resource list? Write up to a one page summary stating why you did not use them.

REFERENCES

Barr, R. & Tagg, J. (1995). From teaching to learning: A new paradigm for undergraduate education. *Change, 27*(6), 13-25.

Characteristics of excellence in higher education: Eligibility requirements and standards for accreditation (2002). Philadelphia, PA: Retrieved February 28, 2003, from http://www.msache.org/pubs.html.

Community College of Baltimore County. (2003). *Guide for learning outcomes assessment and classroom learning assessment.* Baltimore, MD: Author

Kotter, J. P. (1996) *Leading change.* Cambridge: Harvard Business School.

McPhail, I. P. (1998). *LearningFIRST: Strategic plan, 1999-2003.* Baltimore, MD: The Community College of Baltimore County.

McPhail, I. P. (1999). Launching LearningFIRST at the Community College of Baltimore County. *Learning Abstracts, 2*(6).

McPhail, I. P., Heacock, R. C., & Linck, H. F. (2001). LearningFirst: Creating and leading the learning college. *Community College Journal of Research and Practice, 25*(1), 17-28.

Middle States Commission on Higher Education (2002). *Characteristics of excellence in higher education: Eligibility requirements and standards of accreditation.* Philadelphia, PA.

O'Banion, T. (1997). *A learning college for the 21st century.* Phoenix, AZ: Oryx Press.

Wingspread Group on Higher Education. (1993). *An American imperative: Higher expectations for higher education.* Racine, WI: The Johnson Foundation, Inc.

Acknowledgements:

The following individuals at the Community College of Baltimore County were major contributors to this article: Dr. Donna Linksz, Dean, Math and Engineering, Catonsville Campus; Dr. Donna McKusick, Senior Director, Developmental Education; Dr. Rose Mince, Assistant to the Vice Chancellor for Learning and Student Development; Dr. Ann MacLellan, Associate for Learning Outcomes Assessment. In addition the faculty and staff of CCBC deserve high praise for their commitment to improving and expanding student learning.

Henry F. Link, Ed.D., works at the Community College of Baltimore County.

Using the Baldrige Criteria for Institutional Improvement: The Excelsior College Outcomes Assessment Framework

Mitchell S. Nesler
Empire State College – The State University of New York

Over the past 15 years, the outcomes assessment movement in higher education has taken firm hold. Outcomes assessment has become synonymous with continuous improvement, accreditation, quality and accountability in higher education. While scholars have made different attributions about the origins of this movement (cf. Palomba & Banta 1999; Muffo, 2001), there is no doubt that it has helped to change the landscape of higher education. From large public research universities to small private liberal arts colleges, from community colleges to doctoral granting universities, institutions of higher learning are now involved in the process of documenting student learning outcomes for the purposes of demonstrating accountability to stakeholders and providing continuous improvement of the teaching and learning environment.

Despite what should be positive connotations associated with outcomes assessment, the conflict between external mandates (accreditation and state requirements) driving an assessment program versus the internal desire for continuous improvement has been documented (Hjelm & Baker 2001; Muffo 2001). While those in charge of an institution's assessment program should have a deep understanding of the appropriate accreditation standards and ought to have their assessment program include measures to address those standards, the real motivation behind outcomes assessment is the continuous improvement of the teaching and learning environment. Accreditors who follow the spirit of their role are primarily interested in ensuring that the data are collected and used for continuous improvement purposes and in the institutional decision making process. Thus, the goal of continuous improvement should be genuine from an institution's perspective.

Malcolm Baldrige National Quality Award

With its focus on systematic organizational quality, the Malcolm Baldrige National Quality Award (MBNQA) might be the ultimate manifestation of the outcomes assessment movement. Established by law in 1987, the Baldrige Quality Award has historically been offered to business and industry, signifying the stamp of approval of the National Institute of Standards and Technology (NIST). More recently, NIST has made the award available to health care and educational institutions. In the first five years that site visits have occurred in the education category, the Baldrige Award has been given to only one college or university, indicative of the competitive nature of the award. [1]

The Baldrige criteria for education are centered on seven assessment areas (Baldrige National Quality Program 2002):

---

[1] University of Wisconsin – Stout (WI) along with Chugach School District (AK) and Pearl River School District (NY) were the first three winners of the Baldrige Award in the education category. There were no site visits in the education category in 2002 (despite applications from 10 educational institutions). in 2003, the Community Consolidated School district 15 (IL) was the only winner n the educatin category. See http://Baldrige.nist.gov/for details.

1. Leadership
2. Strategic Planning
3. Student, Stakeholder, and Market Focus
4. Information and Analysis
5. Faculty and Staff Focus
6. Process Management
7. Organizational Performance Results

The criteria for higher education require an analysis of the strengths and weaknesses organizations possess on each of the seven dimensions (Ruben 2000). The Baldrige award takes a systems perspective in which the seven dimensions provide an integrating mechanism for evaluating an organization (Baldrige National Quality Program 2002; Winn & Cameron 1998). The Baldrige criteria are based on 1000 points, which are divided up among the seven dimensions. Leadership, which is conceptualized as the dimension from which all others flow, has a value of 125 points. All of the other dimensions have a value of 85 points, with the exception of organizational performance results, which is worth 450 points. The organizational performance results dimension is a direct analog to institutional effectiveness or institutional outcomes, which are conceptualized as the outcomes that follow from the organization's strengths in the other six areas. The weight placed on organizational performance in the Baldrige framework demonstrates the substantial value placed on institutional outcomes, as 45% of the award is based on this dimension. The Baldrige framework integrates key educational themes, such as mission specificity, focus on students, and the concept of excellence.

The relationship among the Baldrige criteria is outlined in Figure 1 below. Leadership, strategic planning and student, stakeholder and market focus make up what is called the "leadership triad," as these dimensions are conceptualized as most directly related to an organization's senior leadership. Faculty and staff focus, process management, and organizational performance results represents the "outcomes triad." Information and analysis, or an institution's assessment strategies, is considered a stand-alone dimension in the current Baldrige model[3] and is deemed a central and crucial part of the Baldrige process. Specific guidelines for assessment include that there must be clear ties between an organization's mission and its assessment objectives. This sentiment is echoed by the Middle States Commission on Higher Education (MSCHE) accreditation criteria (Fernandez, Miller & Suskie 2001; Middle States Commission on Higher Education 2002) as well as scholarship in the area of outcomes assessment (Nichols 1995; Palomba & Banta 1999).

Figure 1

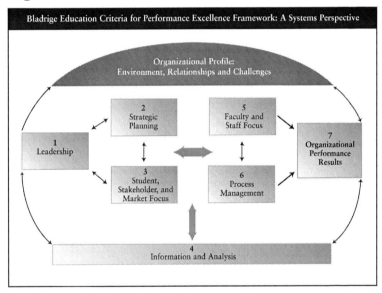

Bladrige Education Criteria for Performance Excellence Framework: A Systems Perspective

---

[3] Winn and Cameron (1998) found that a different model of the relationships between the Baldrige criteria provided better fit with their data than that proposed in Figure 1. This research involved analysis of almost 5,000 surveys of staff at a large midwestern university. Direct relationships were not found between leadership and outcomes, but the relationship between leadership and outcomes was mediated by planning, process management and stakeholder focus.

The first step for Excelsior College in using the Baldrige Criteria was to use the Baldrige assessment during the college's annual strategic planning retreat. Every year, members of the President's cabinet – including all of the Vice Presidents, the Deans, and the Directors of various key functions at the college, hold an off-site day and a half retreat to discuss the institution's long-range plan. During the "Baldrige retreat," the senior administrative staff was asked to identify the institution's strengths and weaknesses using the Baldrige dimensions. This workshop was then repeated for all college staff at unit planning retreats facilitated by deans and unit managers. The results of the two sets of ratings indicated that the Cabinet and the staff overall had similar perceptions of issues related to strengths and areas for improvement at the college. This process allowed for feedback and data collection from both a top-down and bottom-up perspective.

Excelsior College

Excelsior College was the first institution in the region governed by the MSCHE to use the Baldrige Framework to organize its self-study and reaccreditation site visit. Excelsior College, a non-traditional academic institution founded in 1971 amid the early distance education movement in the US, has been working on the cutting edge of outcomes assessment for most of its thirty-three year history. Originally known as the Regents College External Degree Program, Excelsior College is a currently a private, independently chartered institution based in Albany, New York. The mission of the college is to help remove barriers that exist for working adults in their quest for higher education while maintaining rigorous standards of academic excellence. Since its inception, more than 100,000 individuals have earned degrees from this unique college. Approximately 11 percent of the students enrolled in Excelsior College come from New York State;

the remaining 89 percent live out of state and in a number of foreign countries. All of the college's enrolled students (approximately 20,000) are at a distance.

Excelsior College does not have a resident faculty, just as it does not have resident students. Each degree program (business, liberal arts, nursing and technology) has a faculty committee that is responsible for overseeing the curriculum for its respective degree program. The approximately 350 faculty of Excelsior College are drawn from many colleges and universities as well as from industry and health care facilities. They establish and monitor academic policies and standards, determine degree requirements and the ways in which credit can be earned, develop the content for all examinations, review the records of students to verify their degree requirement completion, and recommend degree conferral to the Board of Trustees.

Excelsior College primarily serves a population of working adult students, who for various reasons have chosen to pursue their degrees at a distance (Nesler & Gunnarsson 2000). Most students enroll in the college with a substantial amount of college credit acquired from several colleges and universities. As Excelsior College has no residency requirement, it serves this unique market of individuals who seek degree completion. The college accepts credits in transfer from regionally accredited colleges and universities. While the degree requirements for the college are quite traditional in nature, what is nontraditional about the college is how students go about completing their degrees once they have enrolled.

Once a student has had his or her credits evaluated for their applicability to a degree program, the student will have several flexible options available for completing their degrees. The options available to students are designed to be flexible and self-paced, in acknowledgement of the student's work, family and community obligations. Currency restrictions apply to certain types of credits, such as Nursing or Technology, and may not apply to others, such as general education. To complete their degrees, students will be directed toward distance learning courses and examinations available through the college's Distance Learn database, which contains information about over 20,000 courses and exams from accredited sources available at a distance. Students will also take Excelsior College examinations for college credit; these exams are developed by psychometric research staff in collaboration with faculty content experts. The examinations are delivered via computer at Prometric testing centers and recognized by the American Council on Education for college level credit. Students may also be directed by their academic advisors to take courses at their local college or university to fulfill their degree requirements. Portfolio and other special credit options are available for students to demonstrate proficiency within certain content areas. Evaluation of the credit worthiness of a student's knowledge requires the adherence to higher education guidelines and rubrics. While flexible in its approach, the college makes use of quality assurance frameworks to insure that learning outcomes have been achieved. Given the amount of credit transferred into the college annually, regional accreditation is the most significant quality assurance mechanism used by the college. The college also recognizes the American Council on Education's credit recommendations, PONSI (Program on Non-collegiate Sponsored Instruction) credit recommendations (Hamilton 1997) and certain special programs that have been evaluated by Excelsior College faculty (Peinovich & Nesle, 2001).

The Excelsior College Outcomes Assessment Framework

Given the unique nature of the institution, a strong outcomes assessment program is essential. The outcomes assessment program affords the institution an opportunity to demonstrate to accreditors and other stakeholders that the outcomes associated with an Excelsior College degree are comparable to the outcomes experienced at campus-based programs. As distance education has come under fire in some quarters and its worth has been debated (Nesler, Hanner, Melburg, & McGowan 2001; Phipps & Mertosis 1999; Russell 1999), the importance of solid evidence in support of learning outcomes is greatly valued by the college. To ensure academic excellence, the college utilizes multiple methods and measures to assess program effectiveness and student learning outcomes. Graduate follow-up surveys, employer and supervisor surveys of graduates' competencies, and external faculty review of curriculum and program outcomes are just some of the measures of program effectiveness instituted by the College.

The Excelsior College Outcomes Assessment Framework begins with the college's mission and organizational beliefs:

Excelsior College Mission Statement

Excelsior College affirms that what individuals know is more important than where or how that knowledge was acquired, and believes that students can demonstrate their knowledge and competencies through a variety of methods. The College exists to advance the learning of students, primarily adults, who for personal, economic, family, or other reasons, choose to pursue their education in a flexible, self-paced manner. While remaining open to all, the College ensures academic quality through rigorous programs, student-centered advisement, and careful assessment. By offering high-quality innovative educational opportunities to those desiring an alternative to traditional institutions of higher education, the College strives to broaden individual horizons, develop intellectual autonomy and respect for inquiry, expand career interests and options, and inspire a commitment to lifelong learning.

Excelsior College exists to increase access to education with excellence and economy, particularly for those historically underserved by higher education. The College seeks to meet the needs of a pluralistic society that is increasingly dependent upon an informed and educated citizenry. The College is an international resource and, by example and by advocacy, a major force in expanding access to higher education. As a leader in innovative education, the College works in active partnership with other colleges and universities, employers and organizations to remove barriers to educational opportunity. The College complements the academic offerings of more conventional institutions of higher learning in the interest of equity, economy, and efficiency.

Organizational Beliefs

• What a person knows is more important than how or where that knowledge was acquired.

• There are a variety of valid and reliable methods by which to assess learning.

• The Excelsior College curriculum is designed to ensure that student learning outcomes are comparable to those achieved by students in traditional higher education programs.

• The outcomes of an Excelsior College degree for its students are a function of a lifetime of learning in both formal and informal settings. Since all adults' learning is brought to bear on achieving the Excelsior College outcomes, the College attributes the achievement of all outcomes to its curriculum.

Thus, the institution's mission specifies the expectation that Excelsior College will accept credits in transfer from other institutions. In addition, the college expects to produce graduates with knowledge, skills and abilities that are comparable to graduates from traditional campus based programs. Perhaps most importantly, the college recognizes that the outcomes associated with learning can be assessed in a variety of psychometrically sound ways.

The Excelsior College Outcomes Assessment Framework (Peinovich & Nesler 2001; Peinovich, Nesler, & Thomas 1997) documents the college's approach to student learning. As an assessment based institution serving a population of working adults with substantial college experience, the college does not take a value-added approach to student learning. The concept of value-added, or the "distance traveled" by students, reflects student growth and development during their time with a higher education institution. Value added can be documented with the use of pre-post testing, electronic or traditional portfolios, or via several other methods (Nichols 1995). Excelsior College attempts to demonstrate that graduates of its programs achieve learning outcomes that are comparable to the learning outcomes achieved by graduates at campus-based colleges and universities and is not concerned with growth while students are enrolled. This is primarily because some students may be with the college for a relatively short amount of time, given their credit and experience at the time they enroll; whereas other students may have more to accomplish academically before completing a degree.

The Excelsior College Outcomes Assessment Framework has several assessment goals, which flow from the institution's mission and values and help guide the work to be completed at the college. The assessment goals are as follows:

- Demonstrate that students achieve course and program outcomes, as required by faculty, for each degree program. General education outcomes are assessed at the undergraduate level
- Validate that program outcomes and the curricula are current and as rigorous as those found at other region-

ally accredited United States institutions, and are therefore comparable to those institutions

- Establish that curricula (including general education requirements) are effective at achieving stated program outcomes
- Confirm that the programs are creating access for individuals from a diversity of backgrounds, in accordance with the College's mission
- Authenticate that the institution is effective in helping students from all demographic groups to complete their degrees
- Establish that students are satisfied with their programs and student services

Theoretical Underpinnings of the Framework

The assessment goals of the college were influenced by Terenzini's Taxonomy of Student Learning Outcomes (Terenzini 1997). Terenzini was asked by the National Postsecondary Education Cooperative (NPEC) to assemble a focus group of stakeholders across the higher education spectrum to develop taxonomy of learning outcomes appropriate for the baccalaureate level. The Terenzini taxonomy consists of four sections: educational and training achievement which is academic (such as communication and computational skills, higher order cognitive and intellectual development and content learning); that which is occupational (occupational preparation, job placement, employer satisfaction); that which is developmental (psychosocial development, attitudes and values, and civic involvement); and student goal attainment (educational success, success in transitions, economic impact, and quality of life). Terenzini's taxonomy has been useful to the outcomes framework in that it served to broaden the types of questions posed for longer-term outcomes assessment efforts. The assessment framework also makes use of Bloom's (1959) taxonomy of educational objectives as a framework for organizing cognitive activity. Bloom's taxonomy consists of knowledge, comprehension, and application and higher-level abilities. Ultimately, students are expected to be able to analyze and synthesize the learning from their entire degree in a capstone experience. These requirements for a capstone experience will vary by schools and program.

Assessment Plan

The Excelsior College Outcomes Assessment Framework has a five-year assessment plan, which is updated on an annual basis and reviewed by the college's Academic Affairs Council and faculty. The deans of the college's schools have input on which issues will take priority for a given year, which will in turn have implications for budgetary planning. A long-range plan allows for management of workflow for the assessment staff. Accreditation visits and the accompanying self-study documentation efforts to support those visits are factored into this plan. Certain studies, like large-scale studies examining factors associated with student retention and exit interview studies conducted with withdrawn students, are conducted on a cyclical basis. Other research, designed to monitor program activity and service quality, such as weekly satisfaction surveys for students who have contacted the college, enrollment tracking, and unit productivity reports, is ongoing.

Every program developed at Excelsior College starts with a statement of program goals and objectives. The curriculum for a program is then designed to make certain that the program objectives can be met. These written program goals and objectives provide the map for the assessment of learning outcomes. It is essential for an outcomes assessment program that faculty develop program goals and objectives that are measurable and are meaningfully reflective of a program's curriculum. If critically important objectives are not being met, the curriculum is altered to address the deficiencies. Many colleges and universities do not have formal written program goals and objectives, but it is possible to retrofit objectives to match a program's curriculum. A set of requirements for a curriculum will usually reflect a faculty's expectations for learning outcomes – it may just be a case of providing formal documentation of the faculty's expectations that are indirectly articulated in the curriculum design.

Assessment of General Education

Excelsior College's General Education Faculty Committee revised general education outcomes expectations in 1996, when it was noted by the research staff that the existing 23 outcome statements were in many instances too broad to be measured and were not meaningfully related to the institution's college-wide general education curriculum requirements. When the mismatch between the curriculum and the general education outcome expectations was brought to the attention of the Vice President for Academic Affairs and the Liberal Arts Dean, it was decided to bring the faculty together to re-write the general education outcome expectations. The Liberal Arts Dean and Associate Dean for Outcomes Assessment and Research assembled the General Education Faculty Committee for a two day meeting, with the express purpose of generating an appropriate list of outcome expectations. The Associate Dean for Outcomes Assessment and Research participated to ensure that the faculty developed program objectives that were measurable. It was made clear to the faculty that the curriculum could be changed if certain objectives deemed necessary could not be met by the existing curriculum and that general education outcomes are an aspect of student learning that are subsumed by learning within the major. The group deliberated about the meaning of general education along with examining distribution requirements and samples from other institutions. The result of this meeting was the development of the following nine general education outcome expectations. It is expected that graduates of Excelsior College will be able to:

- Read analytically and critically in a range of fields.
- Write clear, grammatical, and effective prose.
- Think critically in making judgments and identifying and posing solutions to problems.
- Develop cohesive arguments using appropriate supporting evidence.
- Interpret events using more than one perspective, such as historical, economic, biological, social, or global.
- Explain the role of culture in shaping diverse societies.
- Identify elements of artistic and creative expression.
- Apply knowledge of mathematics/natural sciences in different contexts.
- Demonstrate an awareness of the ethical implications of actions.

Based on data from the college's post-graduation survey series, these outcomes expectations were updated in 2001 to include *demonstrate information literacy* as a tenth outcome of the general education core. Alumni in some disciplines were reporting a lack of workplace skills in this area. With the change to the general education outcomes expectations, the General Education Faculty were also considering

---

[3] As of this writing, a learning module and an assessment of information literacy are under development. Students will be allowed to "test out" of this requirement by demonstrating information literacy through a web-based interactive exercise. The learning module will prepare students for the information literacy assessment.

---

how to implement curricular changes to ensure the revised outcomes could be met.[3]

While there are several methods available for assessment of general education, Excelsior College made use of the College Outcome Measures Program from ACT, Inc (Forrest & Steele 1982). The ACT COMP has had a twenty-year history in the US and had been administered by over 700 colleges and universities and taken by over 500,000 students (American College Testing Program 1992). One of the main advantages for using this assessment was the availability of national norms for benchmarking purposes. In addition, the areas assessed by ACT COMP encompass the revised general education expectations for the college. As ACT COMP is a secure assessment, it was necessary to have students participate in secure facilities. A representative sample of seniors was found using mapping software to determine their home addresses in relation to ACT test centers. To insure a representative sample was drawn, 26 testing centers were used that were distributed across the United States (Nesler & Hanner 1998). Excelsior College seniors were invited to participate in this outcomes research and several incentives were offered to encourage participation. Despite the fact that the college mandated that this was a requirement, there was no penalty for nonparticipation.

Ultimately, the most critical issue when drawing a sample for an undertaking of this type is determining if the sample is representative of the population to which the results should generalize. The sample that did participate in the assessment was found to be significantly weaker academically, in terms of GPA and certain examination scores, than the overall population of seniors (Nesler & Peinovich 1998). The sample that participated was also significantly more diverse than the overall population of Excelsior College seniors. Students were found to perform well on the ACT COMP Objective Test during its administration in 1997. Seniors in the baccalaureate programs in technology, nursing, liberal arts, and business scored in the 81st, 77th, 75th, and 62nd percentile, respectively, using national norming data (Nesler & Peinovich 1998). The norming data was provided by ACT and consisted of 27,625 seniors at 86 traditional colleges and universities throughout the United States. Excelsior College associate degree nursing students scored in the 57th percentile compared to second semester sophomores at two-year institutions. Nursing has the largest associate degree program at the college, which is also accredited by a specialized national accreditor, providing the rationale for the inclusion of this group in the ACT COMP assessment (Nesler & Hanner 1998).

In 1998, the ACT COMP Writing Assessment was used to assess students' writing and communication skills. Compared to a national sample of college baccalaureate seniors, a representative sample of Excelsior College associate degree seniors performed at the 74th percentile on the overall test (associate degree norms were not available). Excelsior College Bachelors degree seniors performed at the 86th percentile on the overall test compared to the same norm group (Peinovich, Nesler, & McGowan 1999). Since Excelsior College has open enrollments and no SAT requirements for admission, the a priori expected performance on the COMP measures was the 50th percentile. Since student performance was higher than the faculty's a priori expectations, no actions were deemed necessary by the faculty with respect to the college's general education requirements. ACT has announced they will discontinue the COMP test, so trending of data on this assessment will not be possible. Several options for a replacement measure are currently being explored.

Curriculum Review

The Excelsior College Outcomes Assessment Framework specifies that programs that are not accredited by a specialized national accreditor must be formally reviewed on a cyclical basis. The purpose of this review is to ensure that the curriculum for each of these programs is current, rigorous, and has requirement distributions that are comparable to undergraduate programs nationally. This process involves providing faculty with three sources of information: (1) institutional research data, providing trended information on the headcount, number of enrollments, graduation and retention rates for the program; (2) the recommendations from an external panel of faculty subject matter experts; and (3) outcomes assessment data from surveys of graduates. The information from each of the three elements is presented to the faculty for their deliberations about updating program curricula. Institutional research data helps to frame the scope of the program for faculty members and provides descriptive information. The other two aspects of the curriculum review process will be described in detail.

External Curriculum Review Panel

The external panel of faculty subject matter experts is assembled to compare the Excelsior College program curriculum to that of ten comparison schools, as well as their own institution and what they know about educational trends within their field. The objective of the exercise is to have the faculty unaffiliated with the college rate the rigor and currency of the program, in particular the curriculum requirements. Curriculum currency is assessed against current research and thinking in the academic discipline. In addition, the objectives of the Excelsior College major are included for ratings of attainability, rigor and currency. The ten comparison schools are selected for the entire review process – every major in the Excelsior College School of Liberal Arts, for example, is compared against the same set of comparison schools.[5] The comparison schools were selected based on offering the same set of majors as is offered by the school within Excelsior. In addition, as Excelsior draws students from across the U.S., institutions representing broad geographic distribution were sought, along with a mix of public and private institutions and religious and secular institutions. With the set of comparison schools established, the curriculum for the major under review is evaluated against the major from the comparison institutions.

A rating packet has been developed for this process. Panel members are presented with the requirements for the Excelsior College major displayed in a table side by side with the curriculum for each of the comparison schools. Additional information for each of the institutions, including course descriptions and background information about the intuition, is also included. Rating forms are used to solicit panel member's opinions about the rigor and currency of the Excelsior College curriculum compared to the comparison institutions, as well as their own and general trends within the field.

The external faculty panel is assembled from institutions other than the ten comparison schools, providing additional perspectives to the process. The panel members will also be selected from different institutions around the country, and may represent a different perspective within their discipline than those who originally designed the Excelsior College curriculum. The panel is asked to rate the rigor and currency of the Excelsior College major against each of the comparison schools. In addition, discussion is encouraged surrounding positive and negative aspects of the curriculum at the comparison schools. The end product of this process is a report to the Excelsior College faculty with recommendations for updating the curriculum for the major under review. To date,

---

[5] The Schools of Business and Technology each have their own set of comparison schools, which differ from Liberal Arts and each other. The college's nursing programs are accredited by a specialized national accrediting body and therefore do not undergo this procedure.

---

reviews have been conducted for Excelsior College majors in Biology, History, Sociology, Literature in English, Area Studies, Computer Information Systems, and Political Science. Each school within the college has its own cycle for program review.

Post-Graduation Surveys

Additional data provided for faculty consideration comes from the graduates of the program under review. Research has demonstrated that under the right conditions, self-reported gains can be valid (Pike 1995; 1996). The Excelsior College graduate follow-up surveys were designed to achieve four objectives: to measure current occupational and educational status of the graduate, to measure satisfaction with the Excelsior College education obtained and services rendered, to measure educational outcomes at a time after graduation, and to obtain feedback from employers and graduate faculty about the graduates' competencies. Post-graduation surveys are administered to alumni shortly after graduation (six-months post-graduation), and after some time has past (three-years post-graduation). The rationale for these administration times is so that an assessment can be taken to determine the immediate impact of obtaining an Excelsior College degree, while collecting baseline information for the longer-term survey, as well as getting more proximate feedback on service quality issues. The longer-term survey provides an opportunity to track career mobility for the graduates, as well as their perceptions about their education after obtaining additional work experience with their degrees.

Items on the six month post-graduation survey include: perceptions of the Excelsior College experience; immediate occupational and educational plans; the impact of the degree on their life and career; and the impact of the degree in relation to their original reasons for entering the College. Baseline career information, in terms of personal and household income, job title, and place of employment is also collected. Items on the three year post-graduation survey include: professional development; civic contribution; social integration; efficacy as lifelong learners; achievements in meeting general education and other educational outcomes; career satisfaction, and how well skills learned while enrolled at Excelsior College prepared the graduates for work. The responses for individual students are linked in a longitudinal fashion so that information about their academic careers with the college can be linked to short and longer-term outcomes. The longitudinal nature of the survey research allows for a rich description of the outcomes experienced for students.

As Excelsior College allows students to graduate every month of the year, post-graduation surveys are sent to the appropriate cohort every month – both those who graduated three-years ago and those who graduated six months ago. The surveys include a bar code identifying the individual student – this allows the research office to merge demographic information from the college's student information system with survey response data. This also serves to shorten the survey thereby improving the response rate (Mangione 1995; Tourangeau, Rips, & Rasinski 2000). Each student is sent a series of mailings, including a letter requesting their participation in the research, a letter with the actual survey, and additional follow-ups (Dillman 1978; 2000). Given that Excelsior College produces about 5,000 graduates each year, mail tracking software and a mail service vendor are used to manage this undertaking, as all graduates receive the surveys.

A web-based component is also available for alumni to respond, which is more cost effective, saving postage, printing, and survey processing costs. Response rates have typically ranged from 50% to 75% for the six-month post-graduation survey. The three-year post-graduation survey response rate is lower, given that many former Excelsior College students may have changed their addresses and not updated them

---

with the college. The alumni identify graduate faculty members and work supervisors. These surveys provide additional information for consideration about program strengths and areas for improvement.

Curricular Changes to Strengthen Rigor

With all of this information before them, the Excelsior College faculty can consider making changes to the curriculum for the program under review. In each instance of a curriculum review, recommendations for strengthening and updating the curricula and program goals and objectives have been made by the external curriculum review panel. The Excelsior Faculty have largely adopted these recommendations. For cxample, the Literature in English curriculum was updated to include an Introduction to Literature course as part of the core requirements. The external panel felt that this course would enable students to better integrate subsequent learning. Two semesters of British Literature was reduced to one semester, and one semester of American Literature was increased to two semesters, following educational trends in the field. A new category of elective courses was added, entitled Emerging Literatures (i.e., Feminist Literature, Creative Nonfiction). Finally, while the program objectives were generally deemed "as rigorous" as those of the comparison schools, the Literature in English major objectives were updated to include the ability to write a literary research paper that reflects readings in secondary as well as primary sources and is formatted according to MLA style as a new objective with the requirement of demonstration of this competency. Similar updates have been made to the core curriculum and electives in other majors, as well as adjustments made to the major's objectives.

One theme which has consistently emerged from the curriculum review process is the need for a capstone course that requires students to integrate and synthesize the learning that has occurred over their entire degree. The Liberal Arts Faculty has formed a committee to determine how to best implement a capstone requirement for all majors. Generally, this process has demonstrated that the Excelsior College curricula are as rigorous as those found at other institutions. However, with the passage of time, each curriculum needs to be updated to reflect current thinking within the disciplines, which is why the review process is conducted on a cyclical basis. The curriculum review process used at Excelsior College reflects best practices based on scholarship in the field of program evaluation (Barak & Sweeney 1995; Mets 1995; Nesler & Maynard 2000).

Service Quality

As a focus on the various stakeholders associated with a college is a critical aspect of the Baldrige criteria, and student services at a distance-based institution like Excelsior are a crucial link between the college and its students, Excelsior has paid substantial attention to issues of service quality in recent years. The College's administration has invested considerable time and resources to evaluating and improving student satisfaction with services. The levels and trends in key measures of satisfaction are reviewed and evaluated regularly.

Measures

Satisfaction with the Excelsior College programs and services are evaluated in a number of formal, systematic ways. These include the following:
- Large scale student service quality study conducted by an external vendor (every three years)
- Weekly survey of student satisfaction with service interactions (ongoing)

- Graduate perceptions of service quality at 6-months post-graduation (ongoing)
- Graduate satisfaction with program outcomes at three years post-graduation (ongoing)
- Supervisor survey of satisfaction with graduates' workplace knowledge and preparation (ongoing)
- Graduate faculty survey of satisfaction with graduates' knowledge and preparation (ongoing)
- Exit interviews of withdrawn students in each division (every five years)

The large-scale service quality studies are conducted to provide information that can be used for developing policies and strategies to increase student satisfaction. The weekly surveys are designed to track service quality on an ongoing basis to provide contact feedback about the college's services as they relate to workload and other issues. The short-term graduate follow-up studies (6-months post graduation) are designed to measure graduates' perceptions of service quality shortly after graduation and to establish baseline measures. The longer-term graduate follow-up studies are designed to assess the impact of the receiving the Excelsior College degree and the impact it has had on the graduate's career and other goals. Supervisor and graduate faculty surveys are included as part of this follow-up tracking. Exit interviews of withdrawn students provide another perspective on service quality.

The model of service quality used across all measures at the college utilizes the concept of "service gap" the difference between perceived and expected service (Parasuraman, Zeithaml, & Berry 1994). Five dimensions of service quality are assessed: tangibles (e.g., appearance of physical facilities, equipment, personnel, and communication materials), reliability (e.g., ability to perform the promised service dependably and accurately), responsiveness (e.g., willingness to help customers and provide prompt service), assurance (e.g., knowledge and courtesy of employees and their ability to inspire trust and confidence), and empathy (e.g., caring, individualized attention that the organization provides its customers). These concepts have been adapted to fit with the Excelsior College manner of interacting with students. A Service Improvement Priority Index (SIPI) is calculated based on the gap between perceived and expected services weighted the importance of each factor. The SIPI is weighted by importance so that gaps in areas that are of great consequence to students receive more attention.

The College's first measurement of service quality using the service gap concept was conducted in 1997 in a large-scale study consisting of samples of prospective, enrolled and withdrawn students across divisions, as well as staff members. An external vendor was hired to conduct this research to avoid the appearance of any internal bias in both the development of the survey and the interpretation of its results. Baseline data were collected from students in all programs in an effort to identify service quality issues. Students indicated some large gaps in service quality. As a result of service quality problems identified by the 1997 study, the college undertook numerous service quality initiatives over a three-year span in order to close the "service gap." These included several new services:

- The implementation of toll-free numbers for students
- Providing comprehensive on-line library services
- Offering computer administration of Excelsior College examinations
- The creation of an admissions office to answer pre-enrollment questions
- The addition of a fiscal services ombudsperson to mediate student financial issues
- Making unofficial transcripts available by fax

- The creation of the electronic peer network (i.e., online study groups)
- Providing career resources and information at a distance

In addition to the new services, existing services were improved. These included:
- Enhancement of the college's web site
- Improving the service of the Excelsior College bookstore
- Enhancement of guided learning packages (study materials)
- Shortening processing time for materials to be sent to students

The large-scale service quality study was repeated in the year 2000, after allowing for the implementation of the above mentioned service quality initiatives. The results of the 2000 service quality study indicated that large gains in service quality, as indexed by the large decline in SIPI, were achieved across divisions of the college. The improvements in service quality were dramatic in many areas and could be traced directly to the strategic investments the college made in its services.

The Excelsior College Dashboard

With a comprehensive outcomes assessment program in place, it is necessary to house information in a central location and present it in a readily understandable way (Brown 1996). To achieve this, Excelsior College has made use of an institutional dashboard. The dashboard concept comes from business and industry, where it is used to give managers an opportunity to view critical indices of an organization's progress toward it goals in a concise way. An institutional dashboard is a visual aid, making use of graphics that show trends on critical organizational indices. At Excelsior College, the dashboard consists of six key indicators, developed at a strategic planning retreat by the President's Cabinet. These indicators are *expansion, business results, student success, student satisfaction, productivity,* and *employee satisfaction* (Excelsior College 2002).

Expansion at Excelsior College refers to efforts to access new markets, development of new programs designed to penetrate new markets, development of new products designed to attract new business, and organized attempts to generate new sources of revenue. *Business Results* are consequences of the actions of the college that are related to its mission. At many organizations, business results equate to fiscal performance. At Excelsior, business results include meeting budget and enrollment targets, but also maintaining the institution's accreditation status and providing access to a diverse body of adult learners, in accordance with the college's mission. *Productivity* refers to efficiency of processes, development of expanded services, achievement of benchmark targets for work, for example, achieving an industry standard 95% call completion rate. In many instances, productivity is compared against internal or external benchmarks. Developing new ways of serving students more effectively and expanding student services for existing markets are indicators of productivity. *Student and Employee Satisfaction* are based on the perceptions of those involved. While there are numerous services that the college can introduce that can enhance constituent satisfaction, satisfaction itself is a *perception or attitude* that has to be measured, both in students and employees.[6] *Student Success* refers to any indictor of student accomplishments. These measures include how students per-

---

[6] Introducing a new benefit for employees or a new service for students may be an antecedent of satisfaction, but it is the consequent (perception of the value of that benefit) that is satisfaction.

form on assessments, graduation and retention rates, the types of outcomes experienced after graduation (employment and life satisfaction), job placement/employment rates, pass-rates on licensure exams, supervisor ratings of alumni job performance, graduate faculty ratings of alumni preparedness, continued education/degree seeking, and general education outcome performance.

Each unit and school within the college has its own dashboard that the unit manager or dean shares with the college's President and Vice Presidents on a quarterly basis. The dashboard at the unit level includes productivity, as productivity is more easily measured at the unit level through various reports produced on an ongoing basis. Employee satisfaction is measured at the college-wide level in order to protect the anonymity of employees in smaller units. The consensus on the definitions of the terms was difficult to reach. Some members of the college's senior staff felt that "expansion" was a more desirable term than "business results" to describe their initiatives and there is overlap between some of the categories, such as business results, productivity, and expansion. Items that appear on the dashboard are updated as needed–some items, like indicators of expansion change less frequently. Others, including some measures of students' success and satisfaction, can be updated weekly or monthly. Thus, the dashboard is a dynamic, fluid indicator of organization progress and is formally reviewed at least quarterly by the senior administration at the college. The relationship between the college's dashboard and the Baldrige criteria is clear – all measures of institutional effectiveness are reflected in the dashboard measures. The dashboard is also a example of how

Figure 2

Excelsior College Dashboard

the college makes use of information and analysis, and addresses its primary stakeholders.

Conclusions

Designing an outcomes assessment framework based on the Baldrige criteria was a relatively simple task at an outcomes-based college like Excelsior. The institution has a long history of using learning outcomes to design curricula and examinations, so outcomes assessment was natural extension of the work already underway at the college. Other higher education institutions may require a change in their culture so that stakeholders will embrace information and institutional knowledge generated from an outcomes assessment program. Continuous improvement is generally seen as challenging for higher education institutions as academics tend to resist change. However, a well thought out outcomes assessment plan can be seen by stakeholders as adding value; highlight strengths and creating a mechanism for feedback to faculty and administrators. The Baldrige criteria can provide a useful framework for organizing institutional change and provides a model for continuous improvement in higher education.

References

American College Testing Program (1992). *COMP: Clarifying and assessing general education outcomes of college.* (Technical Report 1982-1991). Iowa City, IA: American College Testing.

Baldrige National Quality Program (2002). *Education criteria for performance excellence.* Gaithersburg, MD: Author.

Barak, R. J. & Sweeney, J. D. (1995). Academic program review in planning, budgeting and assessment. *New Directions in Institutional Research, 86,* 3-17

Bloom, B. S. (1956). *Taxonomy of Educational Objectives*. New York: David McKay Company, Inc.

Brown, M. G. (1996). *Keeping score: Using the right metrics to drive world-class performance*. Portland, OR: Productivity Inc.

Dillman, D. A. (1978). *Mail and telephone surveys: The total design method*. New York: John Wiley & Sons, Inc.

Dillman, D. A. (2000). *Mail and Internet surveys: The tailored design method* (2nd ed.). New York: John Wiley & Sons, Inc.

Excelsior College (2002). *Thirty years of innovation and change: Self-study prepared for the Commission on Higher Education of the Middle States Association of Colleges and Schools*. New York: Author.

Fernandez, T., Miller, P., & Suskie, L. (2001). Goals & outcomes for student learning. Unpublished manuscript, Middle States Commission on Higher Education.

Forrest, A., & Steele, J. M. (1982). *COMP College Outcomes Measure Project: Defining and measuring general education knowledge and skills*. (Technical Report 1976-1981). Iowa City, IA: American College Testing.

Hamilton, R. J. (1997). The assessment of noncollegiate sponsored programs of instruction. In A. Rose & M. Leahy (Eds.), *New directions for adult and continuing education: Assessing adult learning in diverse settings – current issues and approaches*. (pp.31-40). San Francisco: Jossey-Bass Publishers.

Hjelm, M. & Baker, R. L. (2001). Evaluation individual student learning: Implications from four models of assessment. League for Innovation in the Community College Learning Abstracts, 4 (3).

Mangione, T. W. (1995). *Mail surveys: Improving the quality. Applied Social Research Methods Series, 40*. Thousand Oaks, CA: Sage Publications.

Mets, L. A. (1995). Program review in academic departments. *New Directions in Institutional Research, 86*, 19-36.

Middle States Commission on Higher Education (2002). *Characteristics of excellence in higher education: Eligibility requirements and standards for accreditation*. Philadelphia, PA.

Muffo, J. (2001). Institutional effectiveness, student learning, and outcomes assessment. In R. D. Howard (Ed.) *Institutional research: Decision support in higher education.* Tallahasse, FL: Association for Institutional Research.

Nesler, M. S. & Gunnarsson, R. G. (2000). Adult education in the 1990s: An analysis of the 1995 National Household Education Survey database. *Proceedings of the North East Association for Institutional Research,* 143-156.

Nesler, M. S., & Hanner, M. B. (1998,). *Measuring general education outcomes for adult nursing students at a distance.* Paper presented at the Annual Meeting of the National League for Nursing Educational Council, Chicago, IL.

Nesler, M. S., Hanner, M. B., Melburg, V., & McGowan, S. (2001). Professional socialization of baccalaureate nursing students: Can students in distance nursing programs become socialized? *Journal of Nursing Education, 40*(7), 293-302.

Nesler, M. S., & Maynard, A. M. (2000). Curriculum review at a virtual university: An external faculty panel approach. *Proceedings of the North East Association for Institutional Research,* 157-164.

Nesler, M. S., & Peinovich, P. E. (1998). *Using the College Outcome Measures Program (COMP) to measure general education outcomes for adult students at a distance.* Paper presented at the 69th Annual Meeting of the Eastern Psychological Association, Boston, MA.

Nichols, J. O. (1995). *A practitioner's handbook for institutional effectiveness and student outcomes assessment implementation.* New York: Agathon Press.

Palomba, C. A., & Banta, T. W. (1999). *Assessment Essentials planning, implementing, and improving assessment in higher education.* San Francisco: Jossey-Bass Publishers.

Parasuraman, A., Zeithaml, V. A., Berry, & Leonard. L. (1994), Reassessment of expectations as a comparison standard in measuring service quality: Implications for further research. *Journal of Marketing, 58* (January), 111-124.

Peinovich, P. E., & Nesler, M. S. (2001). *Excelsior College Outcomes Assessment Framework.* Albany, New York: Excelsior College.

Peinovich, P. E., Nesler, M. S., & Thomas, T. (1997). A model for developing an outcomes assessment plan: The Regents College outcomes assessment framework. In A. Rose & M. Leahy (Eds.), *New directions for adult and continuing education: Issues in assessment* (pp.55-64). San Francisco: Jossey-Bass Publishers.

Peinovich, P. E., Nesler, M. S., & McGowan, S. (1999, June). *Measuring writing skills at a distance: Using the ACT COMP* Writing Assessment. Paper presented at the 11th Annual Convention of the American Psychological Society, Denver, CO.

Phipps, R. & Merisotis, J. (1999). *What's the difference? A review of contemporary research on the effectiveness of distance learning in higher education.* Washington D.C.: The Institute for Higher Education Policy.

Pike, G. R. (1995). The relationship between self-reports of college experiences and achievement test scores. *Research in Higher Education, 36*(1), 1-21.

Pike, G. R. (1996). Limitations of using students' self-reports of academic development as proxies for traditional achievement measures. *Research in Higher Education, 37*(1), 89-114.

Ruben, B. D. (2000). *Excellence in higher education 2000: A Baldrige-based guide to organizational assessment, planning, and improvement.* Washington D.C.: National Association of College and University Business Officers.

Russell, T. L. (1999). *The no significant difference phenomenon: As reported in 355 research reports, summaries, and papers.* Raleigh, NC: North Carolina State University.

Terenzini, P. (1997). *Student outcomes information for policy-making: Final report of the National Postsecondary Education Cooperative Working Group on student outcomes from a policy perspective.* Washington D.C.: National Postsecondary Education Cooperative.

Tourangeau, R., Rips, L. J., & Rasinski, K. (2000). *The psychology of survey response.* Cambridge University Press

Winn, B. A. & Cameron, K. S. (1998). Organizational Quality: An examination of the Malcolm Baldrige National Quality Framework. *Research in Higher Education, 39*, 491-512.

Mitchell S. Nesler, Ph.D., is the Assistant Vice President for Academic Affairs for Outcomes Assessment and Program Planning at Empire State College, the State University of New York. He was formerly the associate dean for outcomes assessment and research at Excelsior College, where he worked for 9 years.

Assessing Program Effectiveness: Design and Implementation of a Comprehensive Assessment Plan[1]

George B. Forsythe and Bruce Keith
United States Military Academy

During the past decade, various constituencies, including faculty, administrators, parents, students, and the public at-large, have issued calls for more purposive and systematic efforts at managing change in higher educational institutions. Generally, these concerns reflect the desire for integrated models constructed around carefully articulated goals to (a) guide program evaluation, (b) yield data which are empirically valid, applicable, and comprehensive, and (c) manage rather than be driven by change (see, e.g., Ratcliff 1999). Banta, Lund, Black and Oblander (1996) suggest that, in principle, assessment models are most useful to their respective institutions when they are effective (goal-based and responsive), efficient (minimize disruptions and maximize use of existing indicators), and comprehensive (yielding multiple measures at various points in time).

---

[1] We gratefully acknowledge and are deeply indebted to Chris Arney, Casey Brower, Robert Doughty, James Golden, Woody Held, Fletcher Lamkin, Kip Nygren, and Peter Stromberg for their collegial interaction and professional insights.

Assessment models, in reality, often rely on a potpourri of various indicators, many of which provide standardized comparisons of inputs or outputs across institutions. Such indicators often reflect poorly on the resources, history, culture, and networks that uniquely characterize the institutions. Examples of commonly used performance indicators include standardized exam scores, acceptance, retention, and graduation rates, student characteristics such as high school ranking, grade point averages, and national merit scholars, as well as faculty attributes, student/faculty ratios, and program ratings that are partially based on these factors (see, e.g., reviews by Conrad and Blackburn 1985; Tan 1986). In effect, these indicators are used because they are readily available, not necessarily because they represent the best measures of the program's goals. Stringent reliance on such indicators leads to an extreme sort of organizational isomorphism that detracts from the program's goals and yields data typically unable to effectively inform decision-makers in managing the challenges that confront them (see, e.g., Keith 1999).

More recently, higher educational associations, such as the American Association of Higher Education (1992), hereafter referred to as the AAHE, have offered a set of guiding principles intended to emphasize the process of assessment as an important means to more fully understand how the results of outcomes assessments can be used to improve programs. Concurrently, accreditation boards have modified their criteria, placing a greater emphasis on demonstrable accomplishment of programmatic goals. Strategic plans, they argue, should be collaboratively designed by a program's stakeholders in order to guide assessment initiatives, inform decision-makers, and respond to change (Commission on Higher Education of the Middle States Association of Colleges and Schools 1994; Patton 1999). In a very real sense, accreditation boards readily acknowledge the need to learn through application, a point emphasized by both the AAHE and experts, such as Banta, Lund, Black and Oblander (1996). This paper, in an effort to further bridge the gap between theory and practice, describes how one institution, the United States Military Academy, designed and implemented an assessment model, within a specific institutional context, based on the principles offered by the AAHE.

Designing a System for the Assessment of West Point's Academic Program Goals

As the sole institution of higher education in the nation whose primary responsibility is to prepare cadets for a career as professional Army officers, the academic program at the United States Military Academy must provide cadets with an intellectual foundation necessary for service as a commissioned officer. Similarly, in combination with the military and physical programs at West Point, the academic program must foster development in leadership, moral courage, and integrity that are essential to such service. These programs, when taken together, must provide a common experience, based on a core curriculum, for the sole purpose of graduating commissioned Army leaders of character who satisfy the needs of the Army.[2] As such, West Point's academic program is one of several components cadets encounter at the Military Academy, and not representative of all institutional goals and outcomes. This paper will focus only on the design and implementation of the curriculum within the academic program.

The design and implementation of West Point's current academic program is embedded within an historical process

---

[2] The mission of the United States Military Academy is: To educate, train, and inspire the Corps of Cadets so that each graduate is a commissioned leader of character committed to the values of Duty, Honor, and Country, professional growth throughout a career as an officer in the United States Army, and a lifetime of selfless service to the nation.

---

of educational reform dating back to the mid-1980s. The USMA acknowledged four areas of concern regarding outcomes assessment initiatives in their 1989 decennial *Institutional Self-Study* report to the Commission of Higher Education of the Middle States Association of Colleges and Schools, hereafter referred to as Middle States.[3] These included the need to focus on the Academy's goals, the systematic integration of outcomes assessment through comprehensive program reviews, the routine collection of feedback from and about graduates, and the utilization of longitudinal cohort reviews through the management of existing data bases. In response to this report, Middle States recommended the development of more consistent and theoretically based definitions of leadership as the unifying concept for the Academy's programs (academic, military, and physical), outlining how the programs contribute to the accomplishment of the Military Academy's outcome goals. In addition, Middle States recommended the USMA take steps to ensure that the Military Academy's intellectual foundation goal not become overshadowed by the foci of the Military and Physical programs.

During 1990-91, West Point's Curriculum Committee began a review and revision of the Academic Program's goal statements as a precursor to initiating outcome assessments. Members of this committee soon discovered that, while such attempts "fix" the wording of the goals or "reengineer" them by forming clusters of goals, they did little to advance assessment efforts, particularly in the absence of assessment data. In 1991, the Dean, in an effort to implement a curriculum that was both goal based and tied to a systematic assessment review process, established the Academic Assessment Committee, a temporary body, to be staffed by faculty and tasked to build upon the recommendations contained in the 1989 *Institutional Self-Study* accreditation report.

---

[3]See, e.g., United States Military Academy (1989), The Institutional Self-Study, pages 98-99.

As a starting point, the Academic Assessment Committee used the AAHE (1992) principles, as well as other notions of "best practice guidelines", to frame subsequent discussions of curricular reform and assessment. (see an excellent discussion of these principles in Banta, Lund, Black, and Oblander 1996, pp. 3-61). The Committee began with a focus on curricular design, not outcomes, based on the assumption that assessment is intricately linked to curriculum development. A model was designed for the purpose of reviewing the curriculum, leading to a subsequent test of this model on one of the Academic Program's nine goals – the engineering thought process. The Committee succeeded in this endeavor, presenting the results in a 1994 report.[4]

Systematic design of instruction is essential to Army training. The Army's utilization of instruction system design techniques greatly enhanced our ability to incorporate these training practices into a curriculum-design process. Program design, based on curricular goals, lead to the design of a model with four distinct phases. When taken together, the four phases clarify the goal and subsequently integrate curriculum, instruction, and student achievement into a single conceptual framework.[5] These four phases, as presented in Figure 1, include the articulation of a learning model, the design of a curriculum, the design of courses, and the implementation of instruction. As assessment of each of these four phases provides our decision-makers with information on what is to be accomplished (the goals), how it is to be accomplished (the methodology), and the extent to which desired outcomes are

---

[4] United States Military Academy (1994). *The Final Report of the Academic Assessment Committee.*

[5] Institutional accreditation boards that have recently modified their criteria in a manner reflective of this discussion include the Commission on Higher Education of the Middle States Association of Colleges and Schools (MSA), the Engineering Accreditation Commission of the Accreditation Board for Engineering and Technology (ABET), and the Commission of the Computing Sciences Accreditation Board (CSAB).

actually achieved (the results). The model is intentionally structured to be an evolving, iterative, and cyclical process that offers opportunities for faculty development and a periodic re-examination of the goals. Assessment occurs at each of the four phases and includes representatives of all stakeholders.

Curriculum Design and Instruction

We began by specifying a learning model for each of the academic program's nine goals. Our learning models, in essence, serve as a theoretical statement outlining the conditions by which students learn and develop with respect to a particular educational goal. Analogous to a blueprint of the curriculum, the learning model provides a conceptual foundation to guide the selection and arrangement of experiences that are intended to promote goal achievement. Explicitly

Figure 1: Program Design and Assessment as an Integrated System

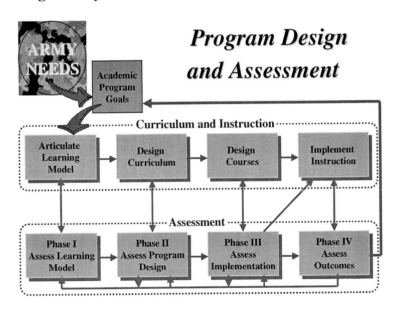

Contexts for Learning

acknowledged in our learning models are statements about the structure, process, and content of the curriculum that will lead to student achievement of an academic goal. The *structure of learning experiences* represents the domain of student inquiry within our professional context. The structural domain serves as a framework to elucidate the areas of study, units of analysis, and the organization of courses/learning experiences necessary to promote cadets' intellectual development. The *process of learning experiences* speaks to pedagogy and represents the activities students engage in to achieve the goal. These activities are organized in a sequential pattern to foster the progression of learning from an introduction of the material through the achievement of the goal. The *content of learning experiences* represents the substance of activities in which students will engage. Content refers to the specific types of information to which students will be exposed that is consistent with the expectations of the military profession. For example, from the large body of knowledge that comprises philosophy, what specific content must be included in the general education of future Army officers?

The learning model is, in effect, a theory about how cadets learn and develop with respect to particular types of educational outcomes. The learning model, as a concept, is a synthesis of three distinct perspectives drawn from the literature on the subject of learning and evaluation. First, structure must be considered, with a focus on student development models and an understanding of the context within which students learn. Second, process must be considered, with an emphasis on theories of learning and instruction. Third, outcomes must be considered, with a focus on programmatic outcomes, which are often oriented toward predictive models of achievement. In principle, the learning model concept integrates these three perspectives in an effort to develop a conceptual foundation that guides the selection and arrangement of students' experiences and promote achievement of program goals. In practice, the pragmatic value of the learning model is that it gets faculty from different disciplines talking about first principles and provides a way to empower faculty while simultaneously promoting curricular integrity (see, e.g., LaPotin and Haessig 1999).

Program design, the second curricular design phase presented in Figure 1, involves the identification of a coherent set of courses or content areas that satisfy the specifications of the learning model. Attention is given to the ordering of these courses and their respective content areas to ensure cadets are uniformly exposed to a logical, sequential learning experience that culminates in the achievement of the academic goal. In concept, articulation of a learning model occurs prior to program design, providing a basis for its organization that includes the selection of specific courses in a curriculum. In practice, courses were, for the most part, already in place when we began this work; program design required an examination of these existing courses to determine which set, when combined or sequenced together, will produce a program that is consistent with the learning model's objectives. A curriculum will conform to the articulated learning model but the degree of specificity may vary from one content area to another.

Course design, the third curricular design phase presented in Figure 1, and implementation of instruction, the fourth phase, logically follow from program design. Course design includes the specification of course goals and objectives, the selection and sequencing of course content, the selection or preparation of instructional materials, the design of tests and other student-evaluation instruments, and the development of instructional strategies and lesson plans. The pedagogy includes instructing and evaluating students, providing them with feedback, and offering remediation. Implementation involves the actual incorporation of these efforts into instruction.

Assessment

The value of the model presented in Figure 1 is that it incorporates both process (how cadets learn) and outcomes (what cadets' learn). The learning model articulates the rationale and amplification of the goal and clarifies what graduates should do with respect to the goal. The program design and instructional implementation develops a process through which cadets learn. Assessment becomes our way of testing, in a scientific sense, the extent to which elements of the process actually accomplish that which was intended. In effect, our four assessment phases are structured to parallel the four curriculum design and instruction phases, through a direct test of the theory (learning model), internal validity (experimental design method), and external validity (real world outcomes).

Our assessment of the learning model involved a separate, impartial, review by a committee whose members were not involved in its construction. As Figure 2 demonstrates, validation of the learning model required a thorough exami-

Figure 2: Assessment of Learning Models

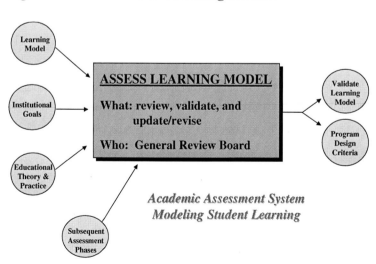

nation of its intent that is combined with a review of the program's goals, educational theory, and application. At a minimum, its assessment involved a periodic review of the learning model in light of relevant educational trends and locally obtained assessment results (based on successive iterations of the process). The committee examined the meaningfulness of the learning model; specifically, critiquing whether the model offers a rational pedagogical structure and process that, when combined with the content of material, is likely to accomplish the program goal for which it was intended. Moreover, the learning model is closely matched, where appropriate, with specific criteria required by the relevant accreditation boards.

Program design assessment incorporates a peer review process to determine if a cluster of courses satisfy the academic goal. Using the learning model as a conceptual framework, our reviewers evaluated the overall fit of the courses with the program goal through an examination of course content and interdisciplinary linkages among courses. As shown in Figure 3, this required a close inspection of syllabi for those courses identified as contributing to a particular academic goal

Figure 3: Assessment of Program Design

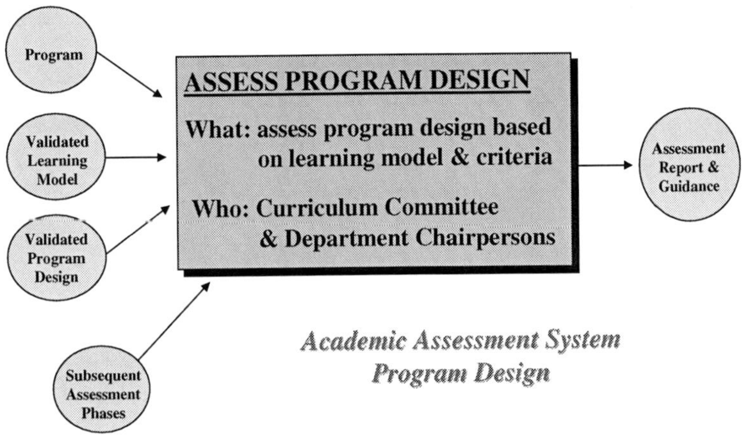

106   *Contexts for Learning*

and a determination of their ability to satisfy the elements of the learning model. The evaluation committee's review, findings, and recommendations were contained in a assessment report to document what has been done in order to provide both strategic guidance to subsequent work and establish a paper trail that documents the rationale for curricular changes.

Beginning with an approved program, the assessment of its implementation involved a review of course syllabi, instructional materials, pedagogical practices, and student assessment methods (see e.g., Angelo and Cross 1993). Assessment methods, as displayed in Figure 4, included an analysis of course products, student surveys, and classroom visitations that are reviewed by faculty and periodically, by peers external to the institution. As with preceding assessments, the evaluation committee's findings were contained within a formal report.

An assessment of goal achievement, what has commonly been termed "outcomes assessment" (Astin 1993; Jacobi, Astin, and Ayala 1987) was designed as the fourth phase in our assessment process. We argue that effective goal assess-

Figure 4: Assessment of Program Implementation

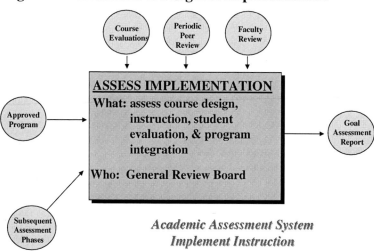

ment requires a learning model be in place, that a program be designed in accordance with the learning model, and that the program be implemented in a manner consistent with the learning model. Without these prior conditions, interpretation of outcomes assessment data is problematic because no conceptual basis exists for making sense out of assessment findings.

To assess student learning and achievement, data are gathered on student performance at several time points. As shown in Figure 5, measurements from several sources were identified as potentially meaningful, to include surveys of students and faculty, student performance outcomes, employer surveys, graduate surveys, and graduates' performance data. Performance outcomes should be more than test scores, representing instead comprehensive indicators of student learning. When strategically embedded within the curriculum, these indicators were thought to provide the most direct measure of achievement, evincing evidence of students' abilities to integrate material and document the program's added value

Figure 5: Assessment of Goal Achievement

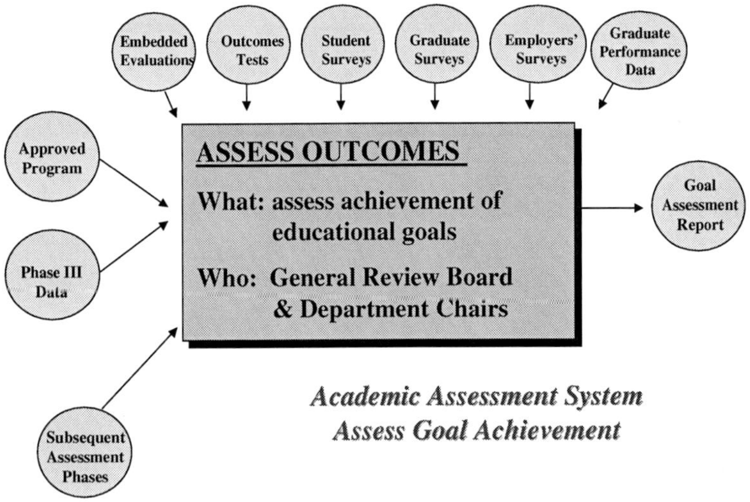

Contexts for Learning

to students' achievements. Insofar as these embedded curricular indicators provide direct assessments of student learning, they will compliment, but not replace, the indirect perceptual indictors obtained via surveys of students, faculty, graduates, and employers. A feedback loop links an assessment of outcomes with a re-examination of the academic program's goals and corresponding learning models. Information gleaned from the model should be used to improve the efficiency and effectiveness of students' learning experience as pertains to the academic program goal. Where disconnects are found to exist in the structure, process, or content areas associated with students' learning experience, attention can be directed to improve the curriculum. Moreover, results from this assessment process can be used to improve the delivery and coordination of instruction through faculty development workshops.

Implementation of West Point's Academic Assessment System

The Military Academy's academic curriculum has two principle structural features. The first emphasizes breadth — a broad set of core courses grounded in the humanities as well as the social, physical, and engineering sciences that, when taken as a set, provide the intellectual foundation essential for career Army officers. This core curriculum, when combined with the physical education and military science programs, constitutes West Point's "professional major." The second feature emphasizes depth – cadets select an academic major or field of study that allows them to study the details of a particular substantive area. Upon completion of the program, all cadets receive a Bachelor of Science degree (as directed by the United States Congress, Title 10, USC, Section 9.02.a).

The correct balance between core courses in the humanities, as well as the social, physical, and engineering sciences is determined, in large part, by the curriculum design and assessment outcomes presented in Figure 1. Once adopted, Military Academy leaders decided to implement the assessment system in phases. We began with goals that related to specific sub-sets of the curriculum, deferring broader goals (e.g., creativity), until we had acquired a greater experiential base. This proved to be a useful strategy because it permitted us to maintain momentum and build confidence as a faculty.

One important recommendation, which emerged from the *Final Report of the Academic Assessment Committee* (1994), was a reorganization of the Dean's staff to "provide an appropriate balance between centralized direction...and decentralized implementation..."[6] The Dean subsequently created an Academic Affairs Division, eventually staffed by an associate dean of academic affairs, an assistant dean for academic assessment, a curriculum specialist, and a clerical secretary. All curriculum and academic assessment matters were subsequently placed within the purview of the Academic Affairs Division.

During the 1994-95 academic year, five academic program goals were selected for review, each of which was assigned to a goal committee; these included goals for (1) understanding human behavior, (2) math-science-technology, (3) historical awareness, (4) culture, and (5) communication. Each committee, chaired by a department head and composed of faculty, was charged with the design and assessment of the goal's respective learning model. The Assessment Steering Committee (ASC), a new administrative body, largely permanent in nature, emerged as a viable solution for the provision of standardizing oversight of the work generated by each of the goal committees; this committee evolved out of the assessment effort and was not chartered or created specifi-

---

[6]Ibid, page 7.

cally by the Dean. Chairpersons of each goal committee served as members of the Assessment Steering Committee (ASC).

In reviewing and, in some instances, restating the academic program's goals, each goal committee was asked to provide a rationale and amplification of the goal's purpose, tied to the Army's needs, and a statement about what USMA graduates can do upon their successful completion of the goal. Members of the ASC utilized a common set of core courses as a curricular framework to ensure that all graduates, regardless of their field of study, held competencies in all subject areas deemed to be essential for the intellectual foundation necessary for officership in the Army. The ASC provided a critical forum for discussion that ensured uniform methods were used to assess the design and implementation of curriculum associated with each goal. In effect, a standard approach evolved, emphasizing the structure (how courses are organized to reach goals), process (how cadets are taught), and content (substantive foci) of the goals' respective learning models. In 1995, the USMA reported in its *Periodic Review Report* to Middle States that it now had a model in place with which to routinely assess outcomes for the academic program's goals.[7]

Four of the five goal committees completed an assessment of their respective learning models by June 1996 and followed in June 1997 with an assessment of the goals' corresponding implementation and outcomes. The committee tasked to assess the academic program's cultural awareness goal identified significant inconsistencies in its curricular design and, after offering specific recommendations, ceased further work until 1998 to ensure that the relevant departments had sufficient time to correct existing gaps in the curriculum. In a manner consistent with the aforementioned pro-

---

[7]United States Military Academy (1995). *Periodic Review Report to the Commission on Higher Education of the Middle States Association of Colleges and Schools,* pages 68-80.

cess, an assessment of the academic program's remaining three goals commenced during the 1996-97 academic year; these goals included (1) creativity, (2) moral awareness, and (3) continued educational development. Following the Academic Board's approval of the new goals, three new goal committees were created and staffed for the purpose of assessing them. The three goal committees completed an assessment of the learning models and curricular design for the respective goals by the end of the 1997-98 academic year. The learning models from each of the nine goal papers were subsequently organized into a single document during 1998, entitled, *Educating Army Leaders for the 21st Century*, which represented the academic program's strategic concept for the pre-commissioning Bachelor of Science degree at the USMA.

The intellectual foundation presented in *Educating Army Leaders for the 21st Century* is balanced with an assessment of empirical evidence to adequately assess how well the academic program accomplishes its mission. Specifically, assessment outcomes must support decisions regarding curricular structure, course design, and course integration. Results derived from assessment initiatives must inform Military Academy leaders how well the academic program is doing in meeting its educational goals, identifying those areas that may require additional attention. The academic program's assessment system is designed to be goal based and responsive to decision-makers, with an emphasis on the use of multiple measures collected at multiple points in time in order to reduce measurement error and increase the validity of inferences about cadets' academic progress. Assessment indicators are selected to maximize the use of existing indicators and mini-

---

[8]The goal team concept parallels the work of Donald Farmer at King's College. For discussion on this subject, the interested reader is encouraged to review Farmer's (1998) text, *Enhancing Student Learning: Emphasizing Essential Competencies in Academic Programs*. 1988. Wilkes Barre, PA: King's College Press.

---

mize disruptions to the academic program's existing functions and structures.

More recently, the ASC replaced the goal committees with *goal teams*, multi-disciplinary operational-level bodies composed of faculty who are brought together to (a) integrate courses within the academic program's curriculum, (b) conduct periodic assessments in accordance with the academic program's assessment system, and (c) monitor the implementation of curricular recommendations that result from such assessments.[8] While, in concept, this activity previously existed in the form of goal committees who periodically reported on comparable information, the nature of the committee structure was oriented toward the completion of short-term assessment tasks. Moreover, the ASC was required to regularly reconstitute a goal committee when it sought to extend the review of a goal beyond a single year, thereby losing valuable time in the implementation of recommendations from the preceding goal committee's report. By contrast, each goal team is now viewed as a permanent multi-disciplinary group of subject matter experts whose orientation is both long-term and continuous. With a focus on long-term oversight, each goal team manages the collection and utilization of data to document the extent to which cadets accomplish the desired goal, identifying any potentially problematic areas in the curriculum.

The goal teams, in conjunction with the ASC determine what changes, if any may need to be incorporated into the existing curriculum and with respect to which specific program areas[9]. Information is also gathered through surveys of cadets, graduates, and graduates' company commanders, as supervisors, in an effort to gather attitudinal indicators (sur-

---

[9]The Assessment Steering Committee is an administrative oversight board, consisting of department chairpersons and administrators, who review, critique, and disseminate the work on the assessment initiatives.

vey data) attesting to the relative strength of developmental programs within the academic program. Officer-performance data, in the form of promotion, retention, and school or command selection board results are also monitored periodically to assess how well West Point's graduates perform in the Army. These indicators, as a set, provide multiple measures of the academic program's nine goals, gathered at multiple points in time, for the sole purpose of assessing the extent to which the academic program's goals are fully implemented into both the curriculum and learning environment. Four indicators have emerged as integral components of the academic program's assessment system.

First considerable attention has been placed on the identification and/or development of assessment indicators that are strategically embedded within the curriculum (see, e.g., Farmer 1999). This involves an assessment of a random selection of students' course products. Criteria must be identified prior to the evaluation of the course products, using rubrics based on the learning model's respective objectives. The rubrics, when taken as a set, serve as a template that can be superimposed on a random sample of cadets' course products (previously described as course embedded assessment). The cadets' projects are evaluated by two or more raters, each of whom use the same template for purposes of assessment (see, e.g., United States Military Academy 1994).[10]. The identification of course embedded assessments has proven to be quite challenging. Some core course projects readily lend themselves to an assessment of a particular goal (e.g., engineering design projects as a measure of the engineering thought process). Other projects have been discovered to have less direct connection to the goals, thus initiating an intensive discussion about the nature of the course with respect to

---

[10]The United States Military Academy found value in this approach when using it as an assessment method in a review of cadets' engineering design projects.

an academic program goal as well as other courses in the core curriculum. Needless to say, we continue work in this area.

Second, the Dean's Office undertook a revision of the First Class survey (a senior survey), which, although it had been collected for many years, was substantially modified during the 1996-97 academic year to more accurately capture cadets' perceptions as they pertained to the Academic Program's revised goal statements and its corresponding learning environment. Administered by the Institutional Research and Analysis Branch of the Office of Policy and Planning Analysis (OPA). Results are used to assess the perceived confidence that members of the First Class hold with respect to their abilities in areas associated with the academic program's nine goals.

Third, in 1997, and concurrent with the administration of the First Class survey, all members of the Fourth Class (first-year students) were initially administered a questionnaire to assess their overall confidence levels in skills associated with the academic program's nine goals. This survey largely parallels that administered to the First Class. Also administered by the Institutional Research and Analysis Branch of OPA, the Fourth Class survey is conducted annually, allowing for an analysis of cross-sectional changes and the establishment of benchmarks. When results of the Fourth Class survey are combined with a year group's corresponding responses to the First Class survey (acquired four years later), the academic program is able to assess longitudinal change in cadets' reported confidence with regard to their skill levels associated with each of the nine goals as well as their satisfaction with the learning environment.

Fourth, beginning in 1997, a USMA working group, consisting of representatives from each of the Academy's three programs, conducted focus group interviews with former battalion commanders located at the Army War College in Carlisle, PA. This initiative, analogous to an employers' survey, provided prompt feedback from graduates' supervisors, identifying how the commanders felt graduates of the United States Military Academy perform, as lieutenants and captains, with respect to the stated goals of the academic, military, and physical programs. Moreover, interviews with the commanders identify, to the extent possible, their perceived fit between the stated USMA program goals and the Army's needs. Battalion commanders who participated in the study consisted of volunteers selected on two criteria: (1) the type of battalion they commanded and (2) recollection of at least two graduates of the USMA who served in the battalion. The focus group interviews are conducted annually.

Two other indicators, presently in the planning process, will, when collected, complete the academic program's assessment system. First, all graduates from a particular year group, beginning with the class of 1996, will be surveyed to assess their perceptions of how well the Military Academy accomplishes its five outcome goals, the purpose of which is to prepare graduates for careers in the Army. The survey will include all active-duty graduates from a commissioned class, administered three years after graduation. Each graduate from the class will be sent a questionnaire to assess their confidence in managing specific skills and attributes associated with the Military Academy's five outcome goals. Responses will be directly compared to their respective responses from the First and Fourth Class surveys, thereby providing a source of longitudinal assessment from the plebe year through three years after graduation. Second, and linked to the first, the USMA is currently undertaking the design and administration of a survey of battalion commanders. Although the results of commanders' focus group interviews at the Army War College offer an opportunity to gather valuable information from Army leaders about the performance of USMA graduates, as focus group interviews, they are not generalizable to the views of Army battalion commanders. This commanders' survey, directed toward graduates' company commanders, will compare commanders' responses to those whom they evaluate (the graduates). The survey of graduates and commanders, intended to be initially administered during the Fall, 1999 and each subsequent year thereafter, will offer multiple perspectives on outcomes of both institutional and program-level goals.

Beyond these data sources noted above, three additional indicators are routinely collected to focus on specific aspects of the learning environment. First, departments are offered an opportunity to bring distinguished professors to the Military Academy, each of whom serve as senior-level faculty for one year. Upon completion of their tenure at the Military Academy, these professors submit a report to the Dean that details their perceptions of the academic program's learning environment. The reports, when examined as a set and over time, provide a trend analysis of common themes. Second, beginning in 1997, the Dean requested an annual survey of the organizational climate. This survey is undertaken to assess the morale and organizational climate of all persons, both staff and faculty, who are associated with the academic program. Indicators are measured and benchmarked to assess the perceived quality of supervision, work autonomy, communication, teamwork, respect for others, work satisfaction, morale, and organizational effectiveness; these represent key components of the learning environment. Third, cadets, upon the completion of each academic course, are encouraged to submit a questionnaire so that instructors, departments, and the Dean's Office receive timely feedback on cadets' perceived quality of instruction. Taken together, these three important indicators represent multiple perspectives of the academic program's learning environment.

Our assessment findings are summarized at multiple administrative levels. At the departmental level, embedded assessments, end-of-course surveys, and course end reports support departmental course reviews, which when combined with command climate survey results, feed into annual program review and analysis briefings of the department to the Dean. At the Dean's (college) level, goal team reports, based on assessments of embedded curricular indicators, surveys of freshman, seniors, graduate, and graduates' employers, in combination with command climate survey data, feed into the Dean's annual program review and analysis briefing to the Superintendent (i.e, President). The intention of these activities is to utilize assessment data at multiple administrative levels for the purpose of informing decision-makers about the courses and programs within their jurisdiction.

When fully implemented, the academic program's assessment system will contain data on graduates as they enter the Military Academy (admissions input criteria), their responses to the Fourth and First Class surveys, and as Army officers, three years after graduation. Learning models for

Figure 6: An Integrated Assessment System

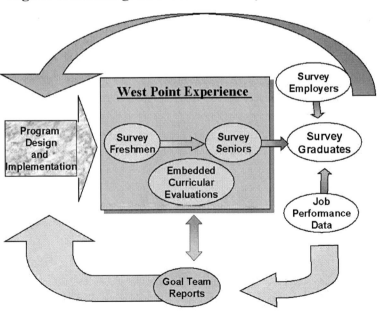

each of the academic program's nine goals and their corresponding curricular structures, continuously assessed by the goal teams, place particular emphasis on the analyses of indicators strategically embedded within the curriculum. The goal teams, in conjunction with the Dean and the ASC, will determine what changes, if any need to be incorporated into the existing curriculum. Information, gathered through a survey of graduates and a corresponding survey of graduates' company commanders, as supervisors, will provide comparable data on the strength of the academic program. Furthermore, officer-performance data, in the form of promotion, retention, and school or command selection board results are monitored periodically by the Institutional Research and Analysis Branch of the Office of Policy and Planning Analysis and provided to the academic program as an additional indicator of how well West Point's graduates perform in the Army with respect to particular goals. These indicators provide multiple measures of the academic program's nine goals, gathered at multiple points in time, to assess the extent to which the academic program's goals are fully implemented into both the curriculum and learning environment. The system, when fully operational, will be organized in a manner that is consistent with that depicted in Figure 6 as shown below.

Lessons Learned

At West Point, assessment is viewed as an integral, planned part of the total academic system, not a nice-to-have accessory. The assessment plan informs and is informed by decisions regarding other academic functions. Assessment outcomes support decisions regarding curriculum structure, course design, and course integration. Similarly, findings aid in decisions about course content and the sequencing of faculty development opportunities. Assessment results inform decision-makers at all levels on how well the program is do-

---

ing in meeting educational goals and direct attention toward areas that may require improvement. While program improvement has primacy, the assessment plan yields meaningful information that can be concurrently used for purposes of accountability. Hence, decisions involving the reallocation of resources can be addressed in a comprehensive manner through a process that involves all relevant stakeholders.

Findings from an assessment of cadets' outcomes are used to continuously improve the quality of the programs. Courses are strengthened by carefully aligning their objects to those of the learning models. Moreover, linkages among the courses become, over time, more closely linked together in ways that are consistent with the learning models. Instructional delivery methods are routinely examined, which offer opportunities for faculty development and reinforcement.

As an example, the academic program's Cultural Awareness goal was impeded by the existing curricular structure. The history sequence offered to first-year cadets is one of the places in the curriculum where cadets are tracked based on their prerequisite knowledge. Most cadets enroll in World History; a few are placed in American History. To accomplish objectives set forth in the Cultural Awareness goal's learning model, cadets placed in American History were found to be distinctly disadvantaged with regard to their knowledge of international cultures. Therefore, the content areas of several core courses were necessarily modified in order to ensure that all cadets received exposure to international cultural diversity.

Outcome assessments also offers opportunities to empower faculty through participation in goal teams; these teams become a way in which faculty take initiative within a multidisciplinary context for the sole purpose of improving the fit of the courses with the goals' respective learning models. This effort serves to foster faculty leadership opportunities and places assessment of student learning directly within the domain of subject-matter experts.

Outcome assessments also enhance accountability concerns. The United States Military Academy is accountable to the United States Congress, the United States Department of the Army, as well as several national and regional accreditation boards. The collection of data, as outlined above, represents a coherent system for documenting program quality. By developing programs that speak directly to the stated needs of the Army and these other constituencies, West Point can account for the quality of its programs at any given time point. In particular, by focusing on programmatic improvement and routinely documenting these efforts, West Point develops a historical record, which acknowledges its strengths, areas requiring improvement, and directions for curricular change. In this regard, accountability becomes a byproduct of program improvement; assessment is seen as an evolutionary developmental process, not a crisis-driven mode of operation.

In sum, the design and utilization of a comprehensive framework offers a feasible application to manage curricular change. The strength of our system is in its integration as an essential component of the academic program, not a nice-to-have accessory. The goals and learning model provide the necessary framework for the subsequent design and assessment of the curriculum. Insofar as the assessment informs policy, the investment in time, energy, and resources is worthwhile. Sub-dividing the system into manageable phases enhances faculty buy-in and maintains momentum. Most importantly, the system is viewed as an evolving process, not as an end-in-itself, for the purpose of continuously improving academic programs.

References

Angelo, T. A. and K. P. Cross. 1993. *Classroom Assessment Techniques: A Handbook for College Teachers*. San Francisco: Jossey-Bass.

American Association for Higher Education. 1992. Principles of Good Practice for Assessing Student Learning. Washington, D.C.: AAHE.

Astin, A. W. 1993. *Assessment for Excellence: The Philosophy and Practice of Assessment and Evaluation in Higher Education*. New York: American Council on Education.

Banta, T. W., J. P. Lund, K. E. Black, and F. W. Oblander. 1996. *Assessment in Practice: Putting Principles to Work on College Campuses*. San Francisco: Jossey-Bass.

Commission on Higher Education of the Middle States Association of Colleges and Schools. 1994. *Characteristics of Excellence in Higher Education: Standards for Accreditation*. Philadelphia: Commission on Higher Education.

Conrad, C. F., and R. T. Blackburn. 1985. "Research on Program Quality: A Review and Critique of the Literature." In, *Higher Education: Handbook of Theory and Research*, edited by John C. Smart. Vol. 1. New York: Agathon.

Farmer, D. 1999. "Course-Embedded Assessment: A Catalyst for Realizing the Paradigm Shift from Teaching to Learning." *Journal of Staff, Program, and Organizational Development. 16*(4) 35-47.

_____. 1988. *Enhancing Student Learning: Emphasizing Essential Competencies in Academic Programs*. Wilkes Barre, PA: King's College Press.

LaPotin, A. S. and C. J. Haessig. 1999. "Fostering Faculty Leadership in the Institutional Assessment Process." *Journal of Staff, Program, and Organizational Development. 16*(4) 49-56.

Jacobi, M., A. Astin, and F. Ayala, Jr. 1987. *College Student Outcomes Assessment*. College Station, TX: Association for the Study of Higher Education.

Keith, B. 1999. "The Institutional Context of Departmental Prestige in American Higher Education." *American Educational Research Journal. 36*(3) 409-445.

Nichols, J. O. 1995. *A Practitioner's Handbook for Institutional Effectiveness and Student Outcomes Assessment Implementation*. New York: Agathon.

Patton, G. 1999. "Outcomes Assessment for Improvement and Accountability: The Role of the State and Regional Accreditation Boards" *Journal of Staff, Program, and Organizational Development.*

Ratcliff, J. L., (1999) "The Rudder and the Sail: Assessment and Staff, Program, and Organizational Development." *Journal of Staff, Program, and Organizational Development. 16*(4) 171-181.

Tan, David L. 1986. "The Assessment of Quality in Higher Education: A Critical View of the Literature and Research." *Research in Higher Education. 24*:223-265.

United States Military Academy. *Institutional Self-Study: Report to the Commission on Higher Education Middle States Association of Colleges and Schools in Preparation for the 1989 Decennial Reaccreditation.* 1989. West Point, NY: USMA.

_____. *Final Report of the Academic Assessment Committee.* 1994. Office of the Dean. West Point, NY: USMA.

_____. *Periodic Review Report: Report to the Commission on Higher Education Middle States Association of Colleges and Schools in Preparation for the 1989 Decennial Reaccreditation.* 1995. West Point, NY: USMA.

_____. *Educating Army Leaders for the 21ˢᵗ Century.* 1998. Office of the Dean. West Point, NY: USMA.

George B. Forsythe is vice dean for education; and **Bruce Keith**, is associate dean for academic affairs. Both are located at the United States Military Academy, West Point, NY.

Course-Embedded Assessment: A Catalyst for Realizing the Paradigm Shift from Teaching to Learning

Donald Farmer
King's College

Excellence in higher education requires moving beyond the mere rhetoric of excellence to implementing successful strategies to develop students as learners. One measure of success can be found when anticipated learning outcomes are established in advance of instruction taking place and when their achievement by students is revealed through assessment measures.

Although many factors contribute to successful student learning, there are two factors that appear to be vital links connecting specific levels of achievement with anticipated learning outcomes. One is to transform students from being passive to being active learners and the other is to make assessment of learning an integral part of the teaching-learning equation. Assessment can play a critical role in developing students as learners if assessment is understood to be formative as well as summative. Assessment best serves as a strategy for improving student learning when it becomes an integral part of the teaching-learning equation by providing continual feedback on academic performance to students. This can be achieved most effectively by designing an assessment model in which assessment strategies are embedded in coursework and intended to be both diagnostic and supportive of the development of students as learners. Assessment encourages faculty to focus on the actual learning taking place for students, and to recognize that teaching and assessment are strategies, not goals.

Viewing teaching and assessment as strategies helps to clarify the confusion over ends and means. The goal for faculty is to produce learning rather than to provide instruction. It is this realization that has helped faculty at King's College to realize the paradigm shift from teaching to learning (Barr and Tagg 1995). The learning paradigm requires a faculty to redefine their role away from being sources and disseminators of information to being facilitators and coaches for student learning. In a learning paradigm students produce their own information, engage in critical analysis, and become creative problem solvers.

Course-Embedded Assessment

Assessment at King's College has been designed to complement the development of a new outcomes-oriented core curriculum implemented in the mid 1980's and was subsequently extended to apply to major programs. The curriculum and assessment models help students to understand the expected exit criteria for graduation and provide a plan by which students may successfully meet these standards. Course-embedded assessment encourages faculty to make goals and criteria for judging student learning explicit as well as developing teaching/learning strategies that elicit sequential behaviors in students that contribute to achieving desired levels of competence.

The King's College course-embedded assessment model

provides a familiar context for faculty in which to implement assessment of student learning outcomes. It focuses on assessing student learning as part of the natural teaching/learning process in the classroom. Although providing common assessment activities for students across the curriculum, it does not in any significant way limit the autonomy of the individual faculty member in the classroom or affect the traditional definition of what it means to be a faculty member. Moreover, qualitative assessment activities designed by faculty for courses taught on specific campus guarantees that assessment reflects what is actually being taught by faculty and being learned by students. Course-embedded assessment also motivates students to take assessment seriously and to perform to the best of their ability since all course-embedded assessments count as part of the course grade.

The course-embedded assessment model at King's College has a variety of components. Course-embedded assessment strategies are reflected throughout the curriculum – both in courses in the core curriculum and in courses in major programs. All core curriculum courses use pre- and post-assessments, common to all sections of a course, in order to evaluate how students think and communicate in each discipline. The assessments are designed cooperatively by faculty teaching sections of the same course. The post-assessment is administered to students two weeks prior to the end of the course in order to provide ample time for faculty to give feedback to students. The post-assessment usually counts as twenty percent of the final examination grade.

Post-assessments need not be comprehensive but rather should focus on a priority goal for the course and reveal the extent to which students can function at a collegiate level within the discipline. For example, in an introductory course in a non-Western culture course, a challenging essay question requiring students to develop and analyze a variety of insights about that culture might be assigned to determine if they have moved beyond the mere information level. Are students able to set aside their own ethnocentrism to reveal a sympathetic understanding of people living in another culture?

Four-year competence growth plans for selected transferable skills of liberal learning provide another component of the course-embedded assessment model at King's College. These skills range from effective writing and speaking to technology and information literacy. Faculty in each major program have developed these plans for their student majors and are reflected in the syllabi of selected courses. These plans include developmental assessment strategies and assessment criteria for evaluating student mastery of transferable skills of liberal learning from freshman through senior levels. Since most students cannot master a skill at the expected level for a graduating senior by taking a single freshman-level course, faculty in each major program must assume responsibility for helping students further develop their skills within the framework of the discipline in their respective major programs. For example, the schedule for assessing transferable skills of students majoring in accounting reveals the choice of subject matter courses in which specific skills are further developed and assessed by building upon the foundation acquired by students in freshman level courses in general education (see Figure 1). Extensive faculty development work has been undertaken to prepare faculty to incorporate student skill development in their courses and to utilize common developmental criteria in assessing student performance.

Sophomore-junior diagnostic projects are another component of the King's College assessment model. The faculty in each major program has designed a project that relates to the major field of study and that can take place in a required sophomore level course. This chronological midpoint in a student's college career is chosen so that faculty and students can discern at this critical juncture a student's likelihood of

Figure 1: Schedule for Assessing the Transferable Skill of Liberal Learning for Students Majoring in Accounting

	FRESHMAN	SOPHOMORE	JUNIOR	SENIOR
CRITICAL THINKING	CORE 100-Critical Thinking	ACCT 260-Intermediate Accounting I ACCT 270-Intermediate Accounting II	ACCT 310-Advanced Accounting ACCT 320-Cost Accounting	ACCT 410-Auditing
EFFECTIVE WRITING	CORE 110-Effective Writing	ACCT 270-Intermediate Accounting II	ACCT 310-Advanced Accounting	ACCT 410-Auditing
EFFECTIVE ORAL COMMUNICATION	CORE 115-Effective Oral Communication	ACCT 270-Intermediate Accounting II	ACCT 370-Accounting Information Systems	ACCT 420-Tax Accounting
LIBRARY AND INFORMATION LITERACY	CORE 110-Effective Writing	ACCT 270-Imtermediate Accounting II	ACCT 310-Advanced Accounting	ACCT 410-Auditing ACCT 420-Tax Accounting
COMPUTER COMPETENCY	CORE 110-Effective Writing CIS 111-Computer Systems and Information Flow I	ACCT 260-Intermediate Accounting I	ACCT 370-Accounting Information Systems BUS 350 or FIN 350-Financial Management	ACCT 420-Tax Accounting
QUALITATIVE REASONING	Math 121-Calculus I	ACCT 270-Intermediate Accounting II – Sophomore/Junior Diagnostic Project	ACCT 320-Cost Accounting	ACCT 410-Auditing – Senior Integrated Assessment

success in the major as well as the student's development of critical liberal learning skills. These discipline-specific projects allow students to work on interesting and realistic problems or projects that reflect the kind of work professionals do in the careers to which students in the major aspire. The project serves as the principal assignment in the course. It is designed at a sufficiently challenging level of to make possible a sophisticated assessment of a student's practice of selected transferable skills of liberal learning and command over the methodology and subject matter of the discipline appropriate for a student major at the sophomore level.

Faculty need to design this assessment activity to anticipate and prepare students to meet departmental expectations on the senior level. Departments initially used the following set of questions to stimulate discussions leading to the creation of sophomore-junior diagnostic projects with a parallel set of question developed for creating a corresponding senior level course-embedded assessments:

- What would you like students to know/be able to do midway through the major? Make a list of competencies, skills, and areas of knowledge you believe majors should have accomplished at this point.
- What criteria could you use to measure accomplishment in these areas?
- In which mid-point course in the major program would you like to assess this knowledge and skills? Why?
- Which assignment currently completed in this course might be refined to assess knowledge and skills? If such an assignment were not currently present, what kind of assignment would be appropriate?
- What would you need to do to develop an existing assignment into a sophisticated assessment project?
- How would this project relate to previous learning in general education and the major program?

- How would this project anticipate and prepare students to meet departmental exit criteria for senior majors?
- What would be the most effective means of providing feedback to students on their performance?

The culminating component of the King's College assessment model is a senior integrated assessment. Within a required senior level course, usually a senior seminar or capstone course, the faculty in each department has created an activity that allows students to demonstrate a sophisticated command over the subject matter and methodology of the major field as reflected in departmental goals for graduates. Students also demonstrate competence at advanced levels for the transferable skills of liberal learning articulated for seniors in the department's competence growth plans.

These assessment activities often include exhibits, lectures, or other kinds of public presentations to which other students, faculty within and outside the major department or even the public at large are invited as audience. Whether as teacher, accountant, journalist, or research scientist, the King's senior completes the academic program of study with a performance that testifies to his or her readiness to function at an effective level to meet the changing expectations of employers in the new Information Age.

Examples of sophomore and senior assessments the Political Science department illustrate the developmental nature of these assessments. The department embeds its sophomore-junior diagnostic project in a required course in public administration at the sophomore level. The instructional purpose of the project is to provide students an opportunity to explore a specific career in public administration. Students select a profession in government service to study by designing surveys, conducting interviews, and doing a literature search. Students then submit a written report and collaborate with peers to present and compare their findings in panel discussions. In addition to assessing student mastery over the methodology and subject matter of political science, faculty also assess students' ability to demonstrate effective writing, speaking, information literacy and critical thinking skills appropriate at the sophomore level.

At the senior level, political science majors build upon their sophomore level learning outcomes and skill development to design research projects in a senior seminar course utilizing primary source materials from an extensive manuscript collection. King's College has the privilege of being the sole repository of the public papers of Representative Daniel Flood, a congressman of national renown who served the 11th District of Pennsylvania for over 30 years. Students must demonstrate their ability to utilize the theory of "home style" developed by Richard Fenno, noted American political scientist, to develop and support a thesis framing their research. Students research Representative Flood's home style in three topic areas: the Panama Canal, Defense Appropriations, and Late 50s - Early 60s Legislation. Students then present their research in writing and orally in a public colloquium. Faculty assess the work of each student according to criteria intended to define the expected level of performance for a graduating senior major in political science.

Role of Faculty Project Teams

Faculty project teams are used to design and manage interdisciplinary courses offered in the general education curriculum and are also responsible for designing and evaluating courses-embedded assessments associated with these courses. Project teams are usually comprised of faculty who are teaching sections of a specific course and are drawn from more than one discipline. General education courses have been designed in the spirit of liberal learning for the non-major and therefore are not intended as the first course in a major program. Consequently these courses do not belong to individual departments. They belong to the core curriculum for general education. Consequently faculty have dual academic responsibilities to their home department and to their general education project team. Project teams operate differently from departments since they are able to focus exclusively on the learning taking place for students in a single course. and the learning taking place for students. Having defined the desired student learning outcomes for the course, faculty are able to focus on assignments, pedagogy, and effective use of class time that best assist students in realizing these learning outcomes. Course-embedded assessment strategies become an integral part of these strategies because a good assessment strategy is a good teaching strategy (Farmer, 1993).

The word "team" has been consciously used to differentiate this group of faculty from the word "committee" that has so many negative connotations among faculty. Whereas most faculty are reluctant members of a committee or are there to protect the territorial interests of their home department, faculty on a project team serve because of their commitment to improving student learning. The spirit and effectiveness of the two groups also are quite different. Whereas a committee usually concludes its work by writing a report recommending that someone else do something, the project team is comprised of doers who are making recommendations to themselves to take action.

Members of the project team design appropriate pre- and post-assessment to be administered in all sections of the course. They also design the assessment criteria that they will use in common to judge student performance. After incorporating the assessment activity as part of the final exam, each faculty number records the number of students scoring on the assessment at the highest, middle, and problematic levels and reports this data to the project team leader. In addition, each faculty member also submits three samples of student performance on the assessment activity at each of the three levels for review by other faculty members on the project team for the purpose of inter-reader reliability based upon the use of common criteria. The members of the project team attempt to identify common student problems and to use these assessment findings as a basis to design strategies to improve student learning. It is these samples of actual student performance on assessment activities, juxtaposed with the criteria used by members of the faculty project team to make their judgments that are retained for review by external evaluators.

The Use of Assessment Criteria

Assessment criteria provide qualitative standards in course-embedded assessment for judging student performance. To guard against excessive subjectivity, it is essential that a common set of assessment criteria be used by faculty to judge student performance responding to a common assessment activity. The two examples that follow illustrate how such criteria help to define expected student learning, integrate skill development with the methodology and subject matter of the specific area of learning, and suggest how course-embedded assessment reflects the idea of the curriculum as a developmental plan of learning.

The first example illustrates the role played by assessment criteria in the pre- and post assessments used in all general education courses. The specific example is taken from a Japanese culture course offered in the global awareness/foreign cultures area of the curriculum. Interdisciplinary courses are offered in a variety of non-Western cultures at King's College. The priority goals for all these courses are (1) to avoid ethnocentrism in developing an understanding and appreciation of the cultural values and patterns of people living in another culture; and (2) to compare and contrast the American mode of thinking, creating, valuing, behaving and communicating with that of people living in another culture. The purpose of the pre-assessment is to understand the prior knowledge base and cross-cultural sensitivity of students enrolled in the course as well as providing a basis for determining the value added reflected in a more sophisticated post-assessment (see Figures 2 and 3). The example for the post-assessment contains two assessment essay questions to illustrate the flexibility in designing such assessment activities while still responding to a common set of assessment criteria.

The second example illustrates the role played by assessment criteria in four-year competence growth plans for skill development that link learning in general education courses with learning in the major program. The specific example is taken from a critical thinking competence growth plan for students majoring in biology. The principal author of this plan is Robert Paoletti, Professor of Biology at King's College. The freshman generic critical thinking course emphasizes critical analysis and extended argumentation. It provides a foundation for biology students to develop in subsequent years more specific critical thinking skills defined by the framework of the biology discipline. This progression can be seen when reading the assessment criteria. The assessment criteria also reveal the developmental model supporting the competence growth plan since the criteria become increasing more sophisticated as a student moves from freshman to senior level (see Figures 4 and 5).

It is not sufficient only to do assessment. Faculty must use assessment findings to engage in continuous improvement. The specificity of assessment findings resulting from the use of criteria makes possible the development of an action agenda to improve both the quality and quantity of student learning. Moreover, samples of student work juxtaposed with assessment criteria can be reviewed by external evaluators in order to engage in a more holistic assessment of student learning by examining actual examples of student performance rather than by relying solely on numerical ratings.

Figure 2: Diagnostic Criteria for Evaluating Pre-Assessments for Students Enrolled in Global Awareness/ Foreign Culture Courses

The faculty will utilize the following criteria to evaluate pre-assessments for students enrolled in CORE 140: Foreign Culture:

(1) Students are able to present accurate information relating to the culture to be studied.
(2) Students are able to see those cultural characteristics and values identified operating in more than one area of the culture (political, economic, social, intellectual, and artistic).
(3) Students are able to avoid ethnocentrism while commenting upon a non-Western culture.
(4) Students are able to differentiate between valid and invalid sources of information.
(5) Students are able to write an essay in which they demonstrate the entry level assessment criteria set forth for freshmen entering Effective Writing (CORE 110).
(6) Students are able to write an essay in which they apply the criteria set forth for freshmen entering Critical Thinking (CORE 100).

CORE 140 Pre-Assessment

One purpose of studying the culture of other people is to be able to compare new information and insights with preconceptions or prior knowledge of the culture before beginning the course of study. As your instructor in CORE 140, I am very interested in knowing about your present knowledge and understanding of Japanese culture. Sharing this information will help me to determine the most appropriate emphasis and strategies to assist you in realizing the goals for this course. Please respond in a thoughtful and specific way to the following writing prompt based upon your present level of knowledge and understanding:

You have been selected as one of twelve college students to travel in Japan at the end of the current semester as part of a student exchange program. Please write a letter to a friend in which you describe your expectations regarding the cultural characteristics and values–political, economic, social, intellectual, and artistic–that you think define Japanese culture.

Please explain the sources for the information and/or impressions you have shared about Japanese culture.

Figure 3: Critera for Evaluating Post-Assessments for Students Enrolled in Global Awareness/Foreign Culture Courses

(1) The faculty will utilize the following criteria to evaluate post-assessments for students enrolled in CORE 140: Foreign Culture:

(2) Students are able to develop a minimum of six insights relating to the specific culture studied.

(3) Students are able to provide specific information for each insight as a means of explaining or providing an example for each insight.

(4) Students are able to compare new information and insights acquired during the course with preconceptions held when entering the course.

(5) Students are able to demonstrate a sympathetic understanding of people living in another culture.

(6) Students are able to demonstrate an awareness of the role played by ethnocentrism as an impediment for understanding people living in another culture.

(7) Students are able to write an essay in which they apply the criteria set forth for freshmen in Effective Writing (CORE 110).

(8) Students are able to write an essay in which they apply the criteria set forth for freshmen in Critical Thinking (CORE 100). CORE 140 POST -AS-SESSMENT

Example #1

One purpose of studying the culture of other people is to be able to compare new information and insights with preconception held about the culture prior to engaging in such a study.

In a carefully constructed essay that reveals both your knowledge base and understanding of Japanese culture, please reflect on the extent to which the learning which has taken place for you in CORE 140 confirms or contradicts your preconceptions about Japanese culture prior to enrolling in this course. Organize your essay according to the new insights you have acquired and provide factual information as a means of providing either examples of these insights or as a means of explaining the basis for such insights.

Example #2

Indicate five insights you have acquired into Japanese culture as a result of taking this course and how they differ from any preconceptions you had at the beginning of the course. Use multiple examples drawn from your knowledge of the culture for each of the five insights in order to illustrate your response, being as specific as possible in your references to the culture. In discussing the examples chosen, indicate how they differ from or are similar to related aspects of American culture. Do not necessarily choose the first five insights that come to mind, but rather choose the most significant among a list of possible insights in order to reveal your understanding of the culture studied.

Figure 4: Freshman Level– Competence Description

Comprehensive Description	Strategy	Assessment Criteria
The student will be able to: 1. Distinguish an argument from a set of claims which are not inferentially related; 2. Distinguish the functions of language to express and influence meaning; 3. Distinguish the kinds and purposes of definitions; 4. Distinguish between validity and soundness as they relate to deductive argument and to evaluate the strength of inductive and rhetorical arguments; 5. Recognize the common fallacies in everyday reasoning; 6. Recognize and assess reasoning in various fields; business, law, science, the arts, etc.; 7. Present extended arguments effectively in oral and written form.	***CORE 100: Critical Thinking*** 1. The student engages in critical analysis and evaluation of extended arguments. 2. The student conducts argumentative essays in which he/she develops a thesis statement with supporting information and/or examples, and validate the conclusion. ***BIOL 111; 112: General Biology I, II*** 1. The student compares the elements of an effective argument with elements of the scientific method paradigm. 2. The student applies the scientific method paradigm to selected reports and laboratory exercises at the introductory level of sophistication.	1. The student demonstrates recall and understanding of the pivotal concepts and processes of reasoning. 2. The student identifies an argument and distinguishes support from conclusion 3. The student identifies language problems, such as ambiguity, vagueness, and emotionally loaded language. 4. The student identifies crucial fallacies in arguments. 5. The student summarizes and reconstructs an argument contained in an extended prose passage. 6. The student draws appropriate inferences from given data. 7. The student recognizes hidden assumptions and implied premises and conclusions of an argument. 8. The student distinguishes subarguments from the main argument in a prose passage. 9. The student separates a problem into discrete units and sets forth evidence in separate, meaningful categories. 10. The student uses the results of appropriate research (library, expert opinion, survey, poll, experiment, etc.) 11. The student identifies and explains the reasoning process applied to various disciplines and demonstrates that process by constructing a strong argument in one of those fields, preferably his or her own major discipline. 12. The student recognizes and performs the basic functions of reasoning. 13. The student chooses and defends an appropriate course of action from among a number of possible alternatives. 14. The student relates an argument to broader issues and concerns. 15. The student evaluates the acceptability of premises, their relevance to a conclusion, and the adequacy of their support of that conclusion.

They can also determine if faculty expectations are sufficiently high and if the range of student performance conforms to the criteria.

The faculty at King's College have learned much about defining and communicating assessment criteria to enhance student learning. Effective assessment criteria need to reflect the following characteristics:

- Communicated to students in writing avoiding ambiguous language.
- Relate directly to faculty expectations for student learning at the appropriate level from freshman to senior year of study.
- Reflect the significant aspects of learning in a discipline avoiding what is trivial or petty.
- Are sufficiently specific in nature to permit student and teacher to monitor progress in building strengths and repairing weaknesses.
- Provide the basis for providing feedback to students and encouraging a continuing conversation.
- Encourage students to engage in self-assessment and to take more responsibility for their own learning.

Assessment as a Catalyst for the Paradigm Shift

When faculty assign a high priority to facilitating student learning rather than merely transferring information, they are demonstrating a behavior that reflects the paradigm shift from a teaching-centered to a learning-centered campus culture. This paradigm shift reflects a significant rethinking of approaches to assessing student learning outcomes that has taken place during the past decade. Two of the most important changes have been the movement from quantitative to qualitative assessment strategies and from summative to for-

---

Figure 5: Sophomore/Junior/Senior Levels–Competence Description

Competence Description	Strategy	Assessment Criteria
1. The student applies critical thinking concepts, principles and strategies, especially those of inductive generalization, hypothetical reasoning and causal arguments, within the context of biological science, and to specific examples therein. 2. The student will be able to apply critical thinking skills to the analysis and evaluation of research papers on a scientific topic at increasing levels of sophistication. 3. The student will be able to use critical thinking skills in the application of the scientific method to selected projects in the laboratory at increasing levels of sophistication. 4. The student will be able to explore a specific topic in a subdiscipline of biology in a manner which would provide preparation for a significant laboratory research project related to the topic and sub- discipline or for the preparation of a written/oral report.	**Sophomore Strategy** BIOL 223: Genetics BIOL 224: Biochemistry 1. The student applies the scientific method paradigm to selected laboratory exercises at the intermediate level of sophistication. 2. The student analyzes and evaluates primary and secondary biological literature sources related to a specific topic within a subdiscipline of biological science at the intermediate level of sophistication. **Junior Strategy** BIOL 335: Vertebrate Biology BIOL 336: Cell and Developmental Biology 1. The student applies the scientific method paradigm to selected laboratory exercises at the intermediate level of sophistication. BIOL 370: Biology Seminar–Sophomore/Junior Diagnostic Project 1. The student applies the scientific method paradigm to selected laboratory exercises at the intermediate level of sophistication.	1. The student demonstrates specificity rather that generality in the use of terms and in the presentation of ideas. 2. The student identifies facts/observations which generate question(s) to be answered by hypothesis testing. 3. The student formulates and/or recognizes and clearly states an hypothesis offered as a tentative answer or solution. 4. The student identifies and clearly states predictions that logically follow, via the deductive reasoning process, from an hypothesis and that are able to be tested. 5. The student identifies and/or devises appropriate sampling and test (experimental) strategies, using proper controls and techniques, to generate data related to the predictions. 6. The student identifies/collects, organizes, and displays qualitative and quantitative data from an experiment. 7. The student analyzes, interprets, and evaluates, using statistics when appropriate, data from an experiment in order to assess its acceptability and relevance as evidence to support or refute the hypothesis being tested.

Figure 5 *(continued)*

Competence Description (cont.)	Strategy (cont.)	Assessment Criteria (cont.)
5. The student will be able to design and conduct original and independent biological research in the laboratory of a faculty member.	2. The student analyzes and evaluates primary and secondary biological literature sources related to a specific topic within a subdiscipline of biological science at the intermediate level of sophistication for preparation of a written/oral report. ***Senior Strategy*** BIOL 430: Ecosystems Biology BIOL 447: Physiology 1. The student applies the scientific method paradigm to selected laboratory exercises at the advanced level of sophistication. 2. The student analyzes and evaluates primary and secondary literature sources related to a specific topic within a subdiscipline of biological science at the advanced level of sophistication. BIOL 490: Biological Research I–Senior Integrated Assessment 1. The student designs and executes a research strategy in order to test a specific hypothesis.	8. The student uses acceptable evidence from the experiments to articulate conclusions 9. The student recognizes and considers assumptions made at any point in the process. 10. The student distinguishes between observation and interpretation. 11. The student recognizes or formulates alternative interpretations that are feasible from experimental results or observations. 12. The student formulates and clearly states support for, or refutation of, an hypothesis by means of the Null Hypothesis. 13. The student suggests further experiments that may provide additional tests of an hypothesis or that may distinguish between interpretations. 14. The student integrates results, interpretations, and conclusions into a conceptual framework or model. 15. The student integrates, where possible or appropriate, knowledge obtained by science with knowledge from other areas of human concern: Philosophical, medical, sociological, economic, legal, moral and ethical.

mative evaluation. Course-embedded assessment speaks directly to combining qualitative assessment strategies with providing formative evaluation. It provides a richness and timeliness for acquiring and actually using assessment data to develop students as learners. Moreover, course-embedded assessment refocuses faculty attention on the actual learning taking place for students rather than on what faculty are teaching.

In an open-ended questionnaire administered to a cross-section of senior faculty at King's College, one faculty member's response captured the sense in which course-embedded assessment has served as a catalyst for the paradigm shift from teaching to learning: "When I became a teacher, I knew that I wanted to help students learn; I soon realized that what helped them to learn were their opportunities to perform rather than my performance as a dispenser of information. I believe that even more now. Because I have witnessed significant student learning as a result of their performances, I am eager to find additional strategies."

Students have also reported in focus group discussions their own sense of the paradigm shift from teaching to learning. They have offered the following observations:

- Sense of faculty support of students as learners.
- Syllabi are more detailed and more directed toward what students will learn rather than what the course and instructor will do.
- Enjoy knowing the criteria that faculty will use to judge student performance.
- Greater awareness by students of their sequential growth and development as learners.
- Increased opportunities for meaningful student-faculty interaction.
- Experience a greater sense of collaboration with faculty and less of an adversarial relationship.

References

Barr, R. B. and J. Tagg, From Teaching to Learning: A New Paradigm for Higher Education. *Change*, November/December 1995, 13-25.

Farmer, D. W., Course-Embedded Assessment: A Teaching Strategy to Improve Student Learning. *Assessment Update*, January/February 1993, 8 & 10-11.

Farmer, D. W. and E. Napieralski, Assessing Learning in Programs. In J. G. Gaff and J. L. Ratcliff, (eds.), *Handbook of the Undergraduate Curriculum*. San Francisco: Jossey-Bass Publishers, 1996.

Donald Farmer is formally vice president of academic affairs at King's Collge.

Assessing Student Attainment in the Major: What's the Question?

J. Fredericks Volkwein
Penn State University

There are two philosophical foundations for assessment: One inspirational, the other pragmatic. **The inspirational goal** is the enhancement of student learning and growth. We in higher education are at our best when we carry out assessment and self-evaluation not to please outsiders, but to satisfy ourselves. Under this philosophy, we undertake assessment not to judge undergraduate education, but to improve it. The goal is to achieve a formative, rather than a summative faculty attitude — an organizational climate of cooperative development and on-going improvement, rather than authoritative finality.

Three questions lie at the heart of student learning outcomes assessment:

1. What should our students learn and in what ways do we expect them to grow? Answering this question requires clear goals and objectives.
2. What do our students learn and in what ways do they actually grow? Answering this question requires evidence and measurement.

---

3. What should we do to facilitate and enhance student learning and growth?

This is the improvement question and requires effective use of assessment results.

Thus, student learning assessment by its nature is goal driven, evidence based, and improvement oriented. Each college or department should set its own particular goals for student learning and personal development, should develop suitable methods for measuring progress toward achieving those goals, and should establish the mechanisms for analyzing, reporting and using the results to improve outcomes in the future. The actual implementation of these assessment activities should be a collaborative endeavor among the faculty, administrators and students. Therefore, assessment is not a product or an end, it is a process or a beginning.

The pragmatic approach recognizes that the 1990s altered forever the context under which institutions of higher education are evaluated in fulfilling their goals and missions. Colleges and universities now face intense pressures to demonstrate their accountability, effectiveness, and efficiency. In an atmosphere of scarcity, those campuses that can measure their effectiveness will do better in the competition for external resources than campuses that cannot. And on the campus, those academic departments that are able to provide Presidents and Provosts with evidence about the impacts they are having on their students will be more successful in the competition for campus resources than academic units not able to provide such evidence.

Both federal and state agencies appear to be holding institutions of higher education more accountable as a condition for receiving funds. The Student Right-to-Know and Campus Security Act , for example, now mandates the reporting of graduation rates, transfer rates, and campus crime. Federal student financial aid regulations stipulate the length of time a student may receive various types of financial aid while attending college, the academic grades he or she must maintain while receiving the aid, and the number of credits that must be accumulated in a given time. Recent amendments to the Higher Education Act require "performance measurement" reports for curricula receiving grants from the Vocational and Applied Technological Education Act (VATEA). Such new requirements come on top of previously existing legislation pertaining to affirmative action compliance, environmental health and radiation safety, and research involving human subjects and warm-blooded animals, among others.

One response to these new accountability regulations and policies has been to debate the purposes of higher education and to focus greater attention on measures of educational effectiveness. As a result, there is growing interest in obtaining answers to traditional questions such as, What should students learn? and How well are they learning it? In addition, the following questions are receiving more emphasis: How does the institution know? What evidence does the institution possess to demonstrate its effectiveness to the public?, and What does the institution plan to do with this evidence to improve outcomes? Such results-oriented questions lie behind federal and state requirements to supply information, and higher education faces difficult challenges in developing measures of its performance.

The ancient Roman God Janus was the God of Doors and Gateways. Like the two sides of a door, Janus has two faces–one looking outward and one looking inward. The classic Janusian challenge for most of us is resolving the tension between the internal and the external uses of assessment and performance. In public and private institutions alike, we face the need to improve ourselves and to become better teachers, learners, scholars, and administrators. To accomplish this, we need to expose our weaknesses and identify what needs to be changed. However, the very act of such openness runs the danger of reducing our market appeal and our resources, especially in an atmosphere of fierce competition and performance funding. But if we are successful in resolving this tension, we will gain a strategic advantage over others.

Thus there are two principal uses of assessment for colleges and universities: the central and traditional use of assessment is as an impetus for **improvement** (formative evaluation); but there is a second necessary use that focuses on **accountability** (summative evaluation). The ultimate goal of assessment is to improve teaching and learning as well as to contribute to the personal development of students. But if we are able to accomplish that goal, we can simultaneously demonstrate our educational effectiveness to external stakeholders and successfully compete for resources.

Various regional accrediting associations, to include the Middle States Commission on Higher Education (MSCHE), North Central Association (NCA), and the Western Association of Schools and Colleges (WASC) attempt to resolve this tension by requiring each campus to present evidence of student learning and growth as a key component in demonstrating the institution's effectiveness. Thus, to be accredited, each of us is expected to gather and present evidence that we are accomplishing our educational goals, that we are promoting student learning and growth, and that we are getting better at doing so. Thus, the accrediting demands by MSCHE, NCA, and WASC properly call our attention to two principal uses of assessment - internal improvement and external accountability. These dual emphases, these twin purposes, seem to offer a constructive path. They provide the foundation for our internal development, at the same time recognizing the need to demonstrate our effectiveness to stakeholders.

Four Assessment Questions

To accomplish these twin purposes, evaluation and assessment force us as professionals to engage in evidence-based thinking. Moreover, the nature of the evidence we gather depends upon the question one asks at the beginning of the process. Most evaluation and assessment activities seek answers to one or more of these generic evaluation questions: Does the student or program meet or exceed certain standards? How does the student or program compare to others? Does the student or program do a good job at what it sets out to do? How can the student's program and learning experience be improved? As drivers for assessment activity, each of these questions - standards, comparisons, goal attainment, and improvement–has advantages and disadvantages that need to be recognized.

Do we meet the standard?

The answer to this question requires what my measurement colleagues refer to as "Criterion Referencing Assessment." This is a form of summative evaluation that is most apparent in the traditional accreditation and certification approaches where students and programs are judged by the whether or not they meet certain standards that have been agreed upon by faculty or other experts in the field. This assessment approach requires definition and agreement about minimum standards or threshold levels of performance. While true scientific measurement is rare, tests of competency and performance skill, quantitative measures of knowledge, licensing exams, and professional judgment methodology are common. While the performance standards for individual students can be locally determined (such as a basic skills test), this type of assessment usually involves the employment of state (the Bar Exam), regional (MSCHE), or national (Medical Boards) standards. Centralized approaches, therefore, are the most common.

There are advantages in using the standards question as the foundation for assessing student attainment in the major field of study. This approach:

- Focuses on ensuring minimum competencies among all students and programs.
- Requires agreement about acceptable levels of performance, thus clarifying the educational and curricular objectives.
- Is useful for making summative decisions about the continuance and discontinuance of students and programs, if that is a necessary task.

The disadvantages of this approach are that such assessment:

- Largely ignores how much students have learned, and few faculty are comfortable disregarding where students started from in the learning process.
- Requires agreement about acceptable levels of performance when faculty may disagree.
- Provides little basis of comparison with performance at other institutions, except on the basis of the percent of students that pass.
- Like pass/fail grading, often makes no distinction between acceptable and top performance.
- If the standard is set externally, undermines the local focus and control of the curriculum.

How do we compare?

Another form of summative evaluation, this approach is referred to as "Norm Referencing Assessment" in the research literature. Performance is judged in relation to that of an appropriate comparison group of students, departments, or institutions. To address this question requires comparative and relative measurement, usually using national or state instruments and norms. Examples might include the E.T.S. Major Field Achievement Tests, Graduate Record Exam (G.R.E.) scores, and reputational surveys. Grading "on the curve" is a form of comparison assessment - each student's grade reflects their performance in the class, relative to others. The following advantages and disadvantages characterize this approach.

Advantages

- Gives opportunities for comparison with students and programs at similar institutions.
- Using national and state comparisons has more external legitimacy.
- Requires no consensus about performance standards.
- This is perhaps a useful approach if one is forced to select or screen a reduced number of students due to limited resources or excess demand.

Disadvantages

- Requires the identification of appropriate normative reference groups and raises the potential of their non-comparability.
- Nationally designed tests may or may not be congruent with local curricular objectives.
- Gives less information about trends and about levels of attainment, especially if the scores are relational (this is a serious deficiency of the GRE).

Are we meeting our goals?

Measuring goal attainment, or "Internal Referencing Assessment," requires clear goals and educational objectives. Unlike the first two approaches, this question requires a more formative student-centered emphasis. This assessment approach often attempts to measure the congruence between goals or objectives or desired performance and actual perfor-

---

mance (or "gap analysis"). The approach uses quantitative evidence only to the extent that goals and objectives can be quantified. More commonly, professional judgment evidence is utilized.

Advantages
- Requires clear goals and educational objectives.
- Recognizes the longitudinal and formative nature of the educational process.
- Is easily tailored to the local curriculum and the needs of particular students.
- Goal attainment is an important and relevant question at every level–individual student, classroom, program/department, and institution.

Disadvantages
- Establishing a clear goal and linking it to measurable performance can be very labor intensive.
- The goal-specific and mission-specific nature of the assessment may not be useful or interesting to external constituencies.

Are we getting better?

The improvement question is the most formative and developmental of all and amounts to self-comparison. This is the one question that is universally applicable to ALL students, institutions, programs, and faculty. Multi-method, multi-measure, and decentralized research strategies are most fruitful, and departments should be encouraged to use a variety of assessment tools and sources of evidence. The following advantages and disadvantages characterize this approach.

Advantages
- Recognizes that institutions and programs and students are at different starting points, and thus is applicable to

all regardless of potential and previous attainment.
- Incorporates a wide and flexible range of objective and subjective sources of information.
- Maintains a focus on the student and the learning process, but adapts easily to a focus on the program or institution.

Disadvantages
- Requires relatively consistent information over time, and results may take years to develop.
- Improvement can be difficult to demonstrate in the absence of a pre-test/post-test methodology.
- Improvement alone may not reflect or achieve satisfactory performance.

As drivers for assessment, these four evaluation questions can be usefully applicd at any level – classroom, program, institution, or system. Regarding the assessment of student development, the four questions also can guide assessment activity and measurement of basic skills, general education, attainment in the major field of study, and student personal and social development. Basic Skills Assessment aims to determine whether students, in the opinion of faculty, possess a threshold level of skills necessary for success in college; and if not, whether instructional services can be provided for those who need them. General education assessment attempts to measure the attainment of intellectual breadth, as distinct from the depth and specialization of the major, in whatever ways breadth and depth are defined by the faculty. Assessing non-cognitive personal development usually taps into student maturity, values, and satisfaction.

While identifying these separate assessment domains, we need to understand how fluid the boundaries are among them–how, in fact, each institution creates an ecologically interdependent environment. For example, student attainment of basic reading and writing and mathematics skills directly supports student performance in general education and in the Major. Further, the educational breadth of a general education program and the intellectual depth of the major are mutually reinforcing. Moreover, students must assume personal responsibility for their own growth in order to meet their responsibilities to the faculty. One's intellectual development cannot be easily separated from one's personal and social development, nor can liberal learning and disciplinary expertness be completely independent.

Nevertheless, institutions usually choose different paths. Congruent with their separate missions, community college staff usually concentrate more heavily on basic skills assessment, faculty at four year colleges often devote greater attention to general education assessment, while faculty at research universities and in professional disciplines are much more interested in assessing student attainment in the major and in graduate programs. The larger and more fragmented "multiversities" usually find it difficult to galvanize faculty efforts in basic skills, general education, and non-cognitive development, but faculty in nearly all institutions can see the benefits of examining student attainment in the major concentration. In the remainder of this chapter, the discussion focuses on assisting faculty with strategies for assessing student attainment in the major field of study.

Alternative Methods for Assessment in the major

At several universities that have initiated strategies for assessment in the major, each department constructs an appropriate means for assessing student attainment using a broad range of possible assessment designs. In some departments where the numbers of majors are small, the faculty might focus on the achievement of all students. Other departments, perhaps with large numbers of majors, may decide to study representative groups of students. The aim of the assessment is not to magnify any particular student's success or failure, but rather to judge, in whatever ways we can, the students' abilities to construct knowledge for themselves and to assess our work as faculty in nurturing, enhancing, and enabling those abilities. Departments might combine some of the elements discussed below, or might design a unique approach, not considered here. Our objectives are to examine what it is students are acquiring when they major in a particular discipline, and to use that information to enhance the learning experience for future students.

Alternatives

Comprehensive Exams

Comprehensive exams can be locally or commercially designed, and there are advantages and disadvantages of each (see Appendix A). When such exams are designed locally by the faculty they have the advantage of being shaped to fit the department's curriculum. Departmental exams have the disadvantages of needing labor-intensive annual revision and local scoring by the faculty, and of lacking a comparison group. On the other hand, commercially designed standardized instruments provide scoring services and more reliable and valid comparison groups; but they may or may not fit the department's curriculum, and are not useful in disciplines wishing to go beyond a multiple choice format. Some departments have attempted to use the GRE score in the discipline as an assessment tool, even though it is generally not appropriate for this purpose. The ETS Major Field Exam (see Appendix B) was constructed in response to the observed weaknesses in using the Graduate Record Exam. The GRE scores are relational, with no subfield scores, and based on a graduate school-bound population. On the other hand, the Major Field Exam scores not only are normed on populations of graduating seniors, and not only indicate the number answered correct (non relational), but also report scores by subfield, thus providing useful information for analyzing the curriculum.

Senior Thesis or Research Project

Such a requirement encourages students to use the tools of the discipline on a focused task as the culmination of their undergraduate academic experience. Under ideal conditions, each department or program uses the student's work to reflect on what students are achieving with the aim of evaluating, and if necessary strengthening, the curriculum and experiences of students within that major.

Performance or field work Experience

Asking students to demonstrate in some practical, or even public way, the knowledge and skills they have learned and acquired, this emphasizes the integration and application of the separate facets of the academic major. Such a requirement may be especially fitting in professional fields like social work and teaching, as well as in performing arts fields. Examples include student recitals, art exhibitions, practice teaching, and supervised field experiences.

Capstone Course

This is usually a required senior course designed to integrate the study of the discipline. It often has a heavy research and writing component. Such courses offer ideal opportunities, both to assess student learning and to strengthen the curriculum of that major. Often the course can contain some other form of assessment, such as a local or national exam, embedded within it.

Student Portfolio of learning experiences

In this mode of assessment, students collect systematically the work that they have undertaken in their study of a discipline. They undertake and write a self-examination of the material, demonstrating how they have constructed the discipline through their writing and thinking over two years of study. Afterwards, faculty meet with students to go over this portfolio. The faculty then could use their own and the students' analyses of portfolios coupled with their perceptions of the student conferences as a basis for conversation among faculty about the curriculum and practices within a discipline. In departments selecting this option all faculty responsible for undergraduate education should be a part of this process, but the plan becomes difficult to implement if each faculty member has to assess overly large numbers of students.

Senior Essay and Interview

The faculty constructs a series of questions that ask students to demonstrate their conceptual understanding of the discipline, and to reflect on the strengths and weaknesses of their programs. The students respond in writing and then meet with faculty to discuss their written statements. The faculty then meet to discuss the results of their conferences with students for the purpose of strengthening the major. Large departments may sample a cross section of seniors rather than the entire population.

Other suggestions:

- **Course embedded assessment** (e.g., standardized examination; classroom research project;
  beginning vs. ending written assignment)
- **Student self-assessment** (e.g., video of oral presentations)

- **Student peer assessment** (builds a learning culture in the department)
- **Secondary reading** of student's regular course work by faculty colleagues (requires an atmosphere of department collegiality)
- **External examiners/readers** (puts student and faculty member on the same learning team — they both want to look good.)
- Using **historical department data** on student performance and placement and course taking patterns.
- Faculty **focus group** discussions with students
- **Surveys of students and alumni using self-reported measures**

Table 1 gives a summary of possible methods for assessing student attainment in the major depending upon each purpose. The suggestions contained in the table should be treated as guides for departmental consideration, rather than as definitive uses. A capstone course or departmental exam might be the most useful for assessing the student's attainment of faculty determined performance standards. For the purposes of meeting professional or national standards, a standarized test or external examiner may be employed. Comparing a student's performance to some external reference group almost always requires the use of a national exam or performance standard, but even graduate school and placement information can be used for comparative purposes. Measuring the attainment of educational goals requires student-centered strategies such as learning portfolios or focus groups or locally designed exams. To answer the improvement question, a wide range of strategies using multiple sources of information can be utilized.

Many exams have been developed by professional organizations in the disciplines such as the Fundamentals of Engineering Exam, the AACSB Business Management Test, the American Chemical Society Exam, the ETS PRAXIS tests for beginning teachers, the National Teacher Education tests in professional knowledge and in various specialties. Some specialized accrediting bodies require exam passage as a condition for professional licensure. In such cases, faculty usually shape the curriculum to maximize student performance. Other tests have been developed by national testing companies such as the ETS Major Field Achievement Tests and GRE Subject Tests, the CLEP-Subject Exams, ACT Proficiency Exams. In addition, to evaluate student attainment in the major many institutions, rely on locally designed exams, course embedded assessments, performance or field experiences, capstone experiences, and self-reported mastery on dimensions that are locally constructed.

By now, it may be obvious to the reader that each assessment question or purpose can be addressed in a variety of appropriate, yet different ways. The question of whether the activity is relatively centralized and controlled by forces outside the department, or decentralized and controlled by the faculty, is perhaps less important than the usefulness of the assessment for enhancing student learning. Even standardized, nationally normed tests can be used by faculty to reflect on the strengths and weaknesses of the department's program. And even the most student-centered form of talent development usually yields results that can be aggregated to serve program evaluation purposes.

There are many appropriate uses and efficiencies to be gained from relatively centralized data collection activities carried out in campus offices of institutional research. Institutional researchers often work with others on the campus to develop and maintain student and alumni information systems that can serve as rich assessment databases. Rather than developing their own survey research, database, and software expertise, departments can draw upon these centralized databases in conducting their own assessment activities.

Table 1: Assessment in the Undergrduate Major Field of Study

Four Purposes	Suggested Strategies and Methods
Meeting Standards	Department Comprehensive Exam Capstone Course with embedded assessment Senior Thesis/Research Project External Examiners/Readers Student Performance/Exhibit with expert judgements Practice Teaching, internships, field work Proficiency/Competency Tests Certification Exams–NLN, NTE, CPA, Medical & Law Boards, etc
Comparing to Others	National Comprehensive Exams–ETS Major field, CLEP, ACT Discipline based exams—Fundamentals of Engineering, Amer. Chemical Society, AACSB, PRAXIS Peer Assessments Program Review by External Experts Comparative Graduate School and Placement Information
Measuring Goal Attainment	Senior Thesis/Research Project Student Portfolio Student Self-Assessment Faculty/student Focus Groups Alumni Surveys Exhibits, Performances, Internships, Field Experiences Capstone Course with embedded assessment Locally designed tests of competency/proficiency

Developing Talent and Program Improvement	All of the Above, especially:
	    Senior Essay followed by faculty interview
	    Faculty/student Focus Groups
	    Course Embedded Assessment
	    Learning Portfolio
	    Alumni Surveys
	    Analysis of historical/archival/transcript data
	    Self-Reported growth

A healthy assessment culture is created when cooperative data sharing occurs between administrative offices and
academic departments. In recent years, a variety of campuses
are able to download from their centrally-maintained student
and alumni databases a variety of useful information that is
helpful to student and program assessment by faculty. The
cost to the institution of conducting separate alumni surveys
in each department and maintaining independent databases
is too high. By surveying several thousand alumni, campuses
can distribute both aggregated and disaggregated summaries
on a wide range of measures of alumni satisfaction, educational outcomes, intellectual growth, career development, and
effectiveness of the undergraduate experience, both departmental and campus-wide.

How One University Responded

In the past ten years, many universities have created Blue
Ribbon Assessment Committees, Panels, Task Forces, and
Planning Teams. Such efforts produce the most enduring results when there is both administrative support and faculty
ownership. At one university, the Assessment Committee
Report recommended that each academic department construct a means for collecting information about student attainment in the undergraduate major as an integral part of a
comprehensive plan of departmental self-study and development. They viewed assessing student attainment in the major
as part of larger curricular review and development efforts
by the faculty.

The Assessment Committee concluded that student
grades in specific courses constitute necessary but not sufficient information about student attainment. Indeed, some faculty give grades based upon student attainment of a certain
standard of proficiency and knowledge; other faculty grade
on the curve; other faculty grade student performance on the

---

attainment of learning goals and objectives embedded in the course; and still others grade on the basis of student effort and improvement. Needed is a more comprehensive view of student achievement in each discipline. In this context, student grades, faculty teaching evaluations, periodic program reviews, alumni studies, and student test scores all constitute complementary ways of obtaining useful feedback in order to improve learning in the major.

In its plan, the Assessment Committee and the Provost recommended a menu of departmental assessment choices, and encouraged departments to design their own if they wished. Most departments submitted plans for assessment in the major and after review and evaluation, some departments began implementation, while others clearly needed assistance in the form of assessment workshops.

Departmental proposals covered a wide range of assessment strategies, including standardized tests, senior research and writing projects, course embedded examinations, capstone courses, student performances and field work, and student portfolios and essays (see the following list). Tailored to suit the needs of each discipline, these efforts gave the University, and especially the faculty, a rich array of information for improving the learning experience of undergraduate students.

After a year or two of experience with one form of assessment, many departments (see the list above) explored another form of assessment, thus adding to the richness of the faculty's collective understanding about the curriculum. One form of assessment evidence shed light on meeting standards, while another reflected student growth or program improvement. One strategy enabled peer comparisons, while another yielded evidence of goal attainment. Judgments of student learning and program effectiveness will be better and richer if they are based upon multiple indicators and measures, and they will be less reliable if based upon a single indicator or measure. A multi-dimensional approach yields a

Results of Department ASSESSMENT Strategies

Senior Thesis or Research Project
Africana Studies (within senior seminar)
Latin American & Caribbean Studies
Women's Studies*
Music (Theory)
Political Science & Public Affairs*
French Studies (Honors)

Performance Experience
Theater (ACT Festival)
Music* (Performance)
Public Affairs (Internship)
Social Welfare (field internship with seminar)

Course Embedded & Capstone Exper.
Africana Studies*
Biology
French Studies
Judaic Studies*
Linguistic & Cognitive Science*
Mathematics*
Philosophy
Religious Studies Program
Women's Studies*
Business Administration*
Social Welfare (seminar with internship)

Comprehensive Examination
Accounting* (CPA Exam)
Chemistry (ETS)
Computer Science (ETS)
German Language & Literature*
Hispanic & Italian*
Social Studies (NTE)
Music* (Theory Exam)
Physics (ETS)
Psychology* (ETS)
Slavic Languages & Literature*
Sociology* (ETS)

Student Portfolio of Learning Experiences
Art (portfolio of artistic works)
English (writing portfolio)

Senior Essay (or Survey) and Interview
Anthropology*
Atmospheric Science*
Classics (joint faculty-student review)
Communication
East Asian Studies (with faculty retreat)
Geological Science & Earth Sciences
German Language & Literature*
Hispanic & Italian*
History
Judaic Studies*
Psychology*
Slavic Languages & Literature*
Sociology*
Women's Studies*
Criminal Justice
Geography and Regional Planning

Alumni Studies and Use of Departmental and Placement Data
Anthropology*
Atmospheric Science*
Biology*
Economics
French Studies*
Geological Sciences*
Hispanic & Italian*
Linguistic & Cognitive Science*
Psychology*
Sociology*
Business Administration*
Accounting*

*Multi-method Combination

far more reliable image of strengths and weaknesses. For example, when a department sees congruence between the information it receives from graduating seniors' test results and from alumni survey results, it has more confidence in the strength of the findings.

Consistent with the Assessment Committee recommendations, most efforts reflected a commitment to ongoing self-reflective development. Departmental plans, with few exceptions, reflected a willingness to make a beginning and to learn from it — to integrate assessment into the department's self-reflective improvement. In a few cases, departments were skeptical and unwilling to undertake assessment in the absence of perfect measures and methodologies. Successful assessment programs on other campuses suggest that perfection is unattainable and that there is much to be learned from getting started, building on the familiar, and developing more informative and effective strategies based on experience over time.

In conclusion, an important ingredient in a successful assessment program is an attitude of cooperation and trust among faculty and between faculty and administrative staff. Faculty need to be trusted to use the information for the enhancement of student learning, and administrators need to be trusted to use the information to promote institutional effectiveness. Assessment evidence should not be used for faculty evaluation. The goal of collecting assessment information should be to promote evidenced-based thinking and new conversations about student learning, and about the curricular experiences that promote student learning.

Appendix A: Pros and Cons of Standardized and Local Instruments

Pros of Standardized Instruments
1. Low initial investment in concept, design and printing.
2. Generally less open to charges of subjectivity and bias (greater perceived legitimacy).
3. Nationally normed for comparisons across institutions.
4. Established validity and reliability –Technically sound.
5. Processing, scoring, and reporting services are available.

Cons of Standardized Instruments
1. No campus control over the content, format, and style of questions. Thus, the test may not reflect the goals and content of your program or curriculum — may measure only a small portion of what is taught.
2. Over time, the test may unduly influence what is taught by faculty.
3. Comparison scores may be based upon inappropriate or unrepresentative norm groups.
4. Less sense of ownership by faculty and staff, and therefore less likely to be used for improvement.
5. May be expensive to purchase and score.
6. May not provide data for follow-up analysis, and will give little information to indicate why some scores are low.

Pros of Local Instruments
1. Reflects the goals and content of the curriculum — it tests what is actually taught.
2. Amenable to a variety of formats (problem solving, essay, performance, etc.).
3. Greater sense of local ownership by faculty, staff and students.

4. Local data enhances additional analysis of results and programmatic uses.

Cons of Local Instruments

1. May have less external credibility and internal legitimacy.
2. More difficult to establish validity and reliability.
3. Lack of normative data for comparisons.
4. Can be costly to design and produce (time consuming and difficult).
5. Scoring and reporting must be locally designed.

Appendix B: ETS Major Field Achievement Tests

Biology

Subscores

- Cell Biology (30)
- Molecular Biology and Genetics (32)
- Organismal Biology (47)
- Population Biology, Evolution, and Ecology (42)

Chemistry

Subscores

- Physical Chemistry (28)
- Organic Chemistry (28)
- Inorganic Chemistry (26)
- Analytical Chemistry (28)

Computer Science

Assessment Indicators

- Programming Methodology (13)
- Software Systems (11)
- Computer Organization and Architecture (12)
- Theory and Computational Mathematics (17)

Physics

Subscores

- Introductory Physics (38 questions): Includes Topics I, II, and III.
- Advanced Physics (32 questions): Includes Topics IV, V, and VI.

(continued)

English Literature
Subscores
- Literature 1900 and Earlier [90-114] Content Categories I-III.
- Literature 1901 and Later [46-60]: Content Categories IV-V.
- Literary Analysis [68-90]: Skill Area 1.
- Literary History and Identification [46-76]: Skill Areas 2-3.

History
Subscore 1
- United States History

Subscore 2
- European History

Subscore 3
- African, Asian, and Latin American History

Music
Subscores
- Theory (70)
- History and Literature (70)
- Style Analysis (56)
- Basic Terminology and Identification (84)

Business
Assessment Indicators
- Accounting (20)
- Economics (20)
- Management (20)
- Quantitative Business Analysis and Information Systems (20)
- Finance (13)
- Marketing (14)
- Legal and Social Environment (13)
- International Issues (12 percent of the questions overlap and are drawn from economics, finance, management, and marketing)

Education
Subscores
* Learning and Development (60-67)
* Curriculum and Instruction (45-52)
* Contexts of Education (30-37)

Economics
Subscores
* Microeconomics (33)
* Macroeconomics (31)

Political Science
Subscores
* United States Government and Politics (34)
* Global Political Understanding - Internat'l Relations & Comparative Politics (52)

Psychology
Subscores
* Learning and Cognition (including Language, Memory, and Thinking) (31)
* Perception, Sensory, Physiology, Comparative, and Ethology (29)
* Clinical, Abnormal, and Personality (27)
* Developmental and Social (34)

Sociology
Subscores
* Core Sociology (General Theory and methodology and Statistics) (36)
* Critical Thinking (35)

Criminal Justice

Assessment Indicators

- Theory (30)
- The Law (30)
- The Police (30)
- Corrections (30)
- The Court System (30)
- Critical Thinking (37)
- Research Methodology and Statistics (15)

Mathematics II (3VMF)

(Current form introduced in January 1999)
Assessment Indicators

- Calculus (15)
- Algebra (15)
- Routine (27-28)
- Nonroutine (12-13)
- Applied (10)

Master of Business Administration

Assessment Indicators (mean percent correct)

- Marketing
- Management
- Finance
- Managerial Accounting
- Strategic Integration

Note for Subscores:
- Reported for each student and summarized for the group.
- Numbers in parentheses are approximate number of questions in each category.
- Overall student scores are reported on a scale of 120-200; subscores (which many of the tests include) are reported on a scale of 20-100.

Note for Assessment Indicators:
- Reported based on group-level achievement in subfields of the discipline Reported for the group only.
- Reported based on the average percent of a subset of test questions answered correctly by all students tested.
- A minimum of five students is required for Assessment Indicators to be reported.

Contexts for Learning

Managing Change Strategies: A Case Study on the Implementation of an Institutional Assessment Plan

Bruce Keith and **James J. F. Forest**
United States Military Academy

Calls for the assessment of student outcomes are now so common in higher education that one might suspect the implementation of an assessment plan is more routine than specialized. And in drawing this conclusion, one would be wrong. We show throughout this essay that the assessment of student outcomes is not a common, universal method, which is easily imported into an institutional context. Instead, student assessment must be adapted to fit the contextual milieu of a specific college or university. Toward this end, we suggest that assessment is neither science nor art but, rather, a practice. While the plethora of literature on the subject of assessment offers guidelines and practical suggestions about frameworks, strategies, and pitfalls, the successful implementation of a comprehensive assessment plan depends upon an appropriate fit with the context for which it is intended.

During the Twentieth Century, higher educational organizations became increasingly characterized by several common features, including infrequent promotion, and informal evaluation, collective decision-making, and individual responsibility. Another feature, lifetime employment, now appears to be partially a myth; according to recent reports from the National Center for Education Statistics, a majority of the new full-time faculty hired for higher educational positions do not hold appointments in tenure track lines (Finkelstein 2002). Nonetheless, given the level of institutional homogeneity apparent in many of these features, one must note with interest that the products and status of institutions are often quite disparate. Such differences underscore the importance of institutional context and, ultimately, the practice of managing assessment plans through the culture of a particular college or university. The view that assessment is a practice is consistent with at least one regional accreditation organization (see the essay by Baenninger and Morse in this volume) and other notable scholars (see, e.g., Banta et al 1996).

Certainly, one would not assume that all colleges and universities are the same. Even within a comparable category such as the community college, schools may vary in terms of their purpose, mission, and linkages to state higher educational systems, differences that may affect the trajectories of their graduates (Keith 1996). Moreover, the type of administrator one brings to a particular school will depend upon the purpose and mission of the institution, the experiences of its students and faculty, the specific organizational networks in place, the level of resources available to manage organizational continuity and change, and the configuration of decision-making structures (Tierney 1991). Although colleges and universities may possess similar structural features, their contextual differences highlight unique configurations of organizational culture. To the extent that culture influences the outcomes of institutional decisions, the successful design and implementation of a comprehensive assessment plan requires one to be attentive to the specificity of institutional context. Any analysis of institutional context undertaken for the purpose of successfully managing change strategies at a college or university will require an understanding of the school's culture. Edgar Schein (1992, p. 12) defines organizational culture as a pattern of shared basic assumptions that the members of an organization or group have learned in their quest to solve problems of external adaptation and internal integration; these assumptions work well enough to be considered valid and, thus, are taught to new members as the correct way to perceive, think, and feel in relation to those problems. Shared cultural assumptions derive their power from the fact that they begin to operate beyond awareness. In this regard, culture is the accumulated shared learning of a given group or organization. For shared learning to occur, Schein (1992, pp. 169-176) contends that a history of shared experiences must persist over time, creating stability, continuity, and predictability in the way decisions are reached within the context of an organization.

William Tierney (1991, p. 130) suggests a framework for assessing organizational culture in higher education. This framework consists of six inter-related factors: environment, mission, socialization, information, strategy, and leadership. The college environment refers to the locality of the school and its historical relationship to that locality. The mission refers to the purpose of the college and its relationship to a decision-making process. Socialization refers to the processes in place at the college, both latent and manifest, which are intended to structure the behaviors and perspectives of its members. Information, strategy, and leadership are reflective of established power structures and decision-making processes within the organization. For example, the successful design and implementation of an assessment plan will require an understanding of how information is developed and disseminated throughout the organization. Strategies require an understanding of how decisions are reached in the college and the willingness or ability of members, such as faculty, to become involved in that process. Implementation of a strategy will require one to identify and work with formal and informal leaders in the organization. Thus, the achievement of a desired outcome within a college or university, such as the successful implementation of a comprehensive assessment plan, will require the skillful management of organizational culture.

Change strategies are more likely to be successful when they are aligned with the organizational culture of a college or university (Kezar and Eckel 2002; Peterson and Spencer 1990). Indeed, institutional culture structures beliefs about teaching, research, curricula, and faculty rewards (Austin 1990) in ways that may contradict disciplinary cultures (Clark 1985). This dilemma adds a source of potential conflict between faculty affiliated with one or more disciplines and their institution. Nonetheless, it is quite plausible, and assumed herein, that the institutional culture will routinely trump disciplinary perspectives because faculty will have greater allegiance, on average, to the institutional culture than to that of their respective disciplines (see, e.g., Gouldner 1957; Forest 2002, pp. 6-12). Thus, as illustrated in Figure 1, the outcomes of proposed change strategies within an institution will require a well-articulated vision (purpose), senior administrative support (leadership), collaborative leadership strategies (informed decision-making), and professional development (socialization).

Senior administrators will necessarily have to support a proposed change strategy before it can be successfully implemented at the institution. Grassroots movements supportive of a change strategy may provide the impetus for deliberation of an issue, but without administrative support the issue is unlikely to be successfully implemented. Moreover, the purpose of the proposed change must be clearly articulated, at least to those persons who are participants in the decision-making process. An autocratic, highly centralized decision-making authority may not require faculty to be directly involved in the deliberations, while an organization with a more decentralized leadership structure may not be able to entertain change strategies without the direct consent of some faculty. When the issue in question involves the implementation of a comprehensive assessment plan requiring faculty involvement in order to successfully assess student outcomes, the faculty will need to become participants in the process. In the case of the autocratic structure, the decision to implement

Figure 1: Managing Change Strategies within Institutional Contexts

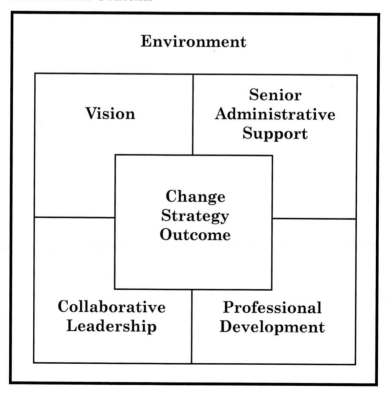

may occur at a senior administrative level with faculty given incentives to participate in the process. By contrast, in a college structured by a collaborative decision-making authority, faculty accustomed to being involved in decisions of change strategies may actually block implementation through socialization efforts (a lack of buy-in) and defensive strategies (lack of participation) if not initially included as full participants in the decision-making process. In both instances, outcomes will vary depending upon the contextual features associated with institutional cultures.

Managing Change Strategies at the United States Military Academy

Implementation of a change strategy requires careful attention to a number of contextual factors within the institution. These include a focus on environment, vision, senior administrative support, collaborative leadership strategies, and professional development.

Throughout the remainder of our paper, we discuss the relevance of each of these features to the successful implementation of a comprehensive assessment plan at the United States Military Academy.

Environment

The service academies are unique members of the higher educational landscape in the United States. As training grounds for future officers of the nationís armed forces, each service academy is dedicated to the highest standards of academic, military, and physical education. The students (cadets) who attend these institutions are uniquely dedicated to the principles of service and discipline, and are among the most accomplished high school graduates attending any tertiary institution in the United States.

The first year of student life at West Point is unlike that found at virtually any civilian college or university in the country. An extremely organized regimen of memorization, drill, physical development and discipline prepares these young men and women for life in the military. Steeped in rules and regulations and continuously challenged in the classroom and the military training grounds, freshmen must quickly learn to establish priorities and manage their time effectively. Throughout their four-year experience, cadets develop as leaders, taking on roles of increasing responsibility as peer guides and mentors for less experienced cadets.

During the past two centuries, the Military Academy has been organized to ensure that senior administrators and faculty ought to consist of seasoned military officers. Thus, the Military Academy has historically relied on a set of rotating military faculty–those identified as highly promotable and self-directed learners. Once selected, these officers are sent, at government expense, to prominent universities in the country to pursue a graduate degree, typically at the master's level, in their selected field. In return for this educational opportunity, they spend an average of three years as instructors at West Point. Following this tour, they return to the Army, where they assume new leadership positions in the Army. The assumption underlying this strategy is based on a belief that field experience, when combined with in-depth knowledge of a field, is the best form of role modeling available to the cadets. Rotating faculty constitute approximately two-thirds of all faculty at the Military Academy.

Civilian faculty, particularly those with no prior military experience, are a recent introduction to the Military Academy. Mandated by Congress in the early 1990s, the civilian faculty serve as a group of subject-matter experts who are expected to provide the institutional history and continuity largely lost in the rotation of military faculty (National Defense Authorization Act 1993). Civilians presently constitute approximately 21 percent of the Military Academy's faculty. The remaining 14 percent of the faculty are senior military officers.

Vision

A central goal of the Military Academy is to provide the nation with leaders of character. A leader of character not only has the knowledge of what is right, but also the moral courage to act on that knowledge (United States Military Academy 2001). The cadet honor code at West Point is similar to that of the other academies: "A cadet will not lie, cheat, steal, nor tolerate among us anyone who does." Students, faculty and staff are held to the highest standards of behavior, and the response to violations of this ethical code can include suspension or prompt dismissal of students or civilians, and possibly even court-martial for members of the armed services.

The enforcement of a strict moral code is meant to ensure clarity and ethical reasoning in the Military Academy's graduates. Duty, a commitment to self-less service, courage, honesty, loyalty, punctuality, and teamwork comprise the core of a cadet's experience. The concept of personal and professional honor permeates life at West Point and, when combined with a student population of over-achievers, leads to a uniquely exciting learning environment. Indeed, West Point has a considerable advantage over many other collegesóthey can be very selective in their admissions procedures, and have a great deal of latitude to choose candidates who have demonstrated strong ethical and moral qualities and who will potentially make significant contributions to the Army.

Strategic guidance from the Department of Defense and the Army serves as the basis for deciding the mission and goals of the Military Academy. The academic curriculum is structured to ensure that the Military Academy's graduates can anticipate and respond effectively to the uncertainties of the changing world they are likely to encounter as Army officers. They will confront challenges, problems, opportunities, and military threats with confidence in their abilities to accomplish their assigned missions. Graduates will be able to survey the social, political, economic, and technological environment to identify new ideas and trends and imagine the range of possible consequences these changes have for the Army and the Nation.

As they prepare to meet the demands of the future, the Military Academy's graduates must recognize the breadth, depth, and limits of their own knowledge and be confident in their ability to undertake self-directed, independent study to meet the challenges that confront them. They must be able to communicate ideas and insights and draw generalizations and inferences about world events. Moreover, graduates must recognize and appreciate diverse perspectives on complex situations, and employ an interdisciplinary approach to understanding the causes of the challenges they face and the consequences of their actions.

Senior Administrative Support

The senior administration at the Military Academy consists of the Superintendent, Dean of the Academic Board, and the Commandant of Cadets. The Superintendent is the college CEO, whereas the Dean is the chief academic officer and the Commandant manages military and physical education. Together, they constitute the leader teamómost comparable to positions that one would find at other colleges as the president, an academic dean, and dean of students.

The Superintendent wears two hats simultaneously–one of a college president and the other as a senior military officer. In the civilian world, college presidents are chosen through a lengthy process involving professional search firms, faculty committees, and trustees or governing board members. At the Military Academy, the Superintendent is chosen by the Department of the Army and approved by Congress. The USMA Superintendent holds the military rank of lieutenant general (three stars) and has spent nearly his entire career in the field, having served as battalion and brigade commanders and as a senior staff member for the Army chief. Superintendents serve for a fixed five-year obligation; they are expected to retire from the Army following completion of this duty. The short five-year interval often brings Superintendents to West Point with a distinct vision and a set of priorities. This, in turn, can affect institutional direction, resource allocation, administrative policies, scheduling, and perhaps most importantly, the cadet experience.

Similar to most higher educational institutions, the academic program at West Point is led by a Dean, typically an individual whose academic credentials and leadership experience will command the respect of faculty throughout the institution. The Dean is drawn from among the 13 academic departments, having previously served as a professor of discipline and department head. Upon appointment to the position of Dean, he is promoted from colonel to brigadier general (one star). His term as Dean is limited to five years and, as with the Superintendent, he is expected to retire from the Army following this tour of duty. The Dean is responsible for managing the curriculum, assessment, and accreditation of the academic program as well as the management of all resources that affect these areas.

The Commandant of Cadets possesses an experiential base that is quite distinct from that of the Dean and, to a lesser extent, the Superintendent. He has recently been promoted to brigadier general and is given a typical term of 18 to 24 months to mange cadets' military and physical education programs. His focus is extremely short-term, largely intended to ensure an alignment between the Army and the military program. Unlike the Superintendent and Dean, the Commandant is on an upwardly mobile career trajectory; he will be assigned to a new command in the Army and receive a promotion to major general (two stars) when he assumes the duties of that command.

These three senior administrative leaders have a genuine focus on the military. The Dean is expected to ensure that the academic curriculum is aligned with both the Army's needs and higher educational standards. As brigadier generals, the Dean and Commandant hold an equal status. Disagreements between them involving issues of cadet time and load must be resolved by the Superintendent. Yet, as president, the Superintendent is often focused on external concerns of the Military Academy, including endowments, resource distributions through Congressional and Department of the Army channels, and infrastructure development. Absent from the leader team is a senior administrative officer who oversees all internal matters concerning the three programsóacademic, military, physicalóand management of cadet time. In comparison to other colleges and universities, the USMA senior administrative structure lacks a provost.

Collaborative Leadership Strategies

Faculty governance at West Point is concentrated primarily through 15 individuals, each of whom serve as the head of a department. The Military Academy has 13 academic departments, a department of military instruction, and a department of physical education. The Dean oversees the academic departments while the Commandant manages the departments of military and physical education. These 15 individuals, along with the Superintendent, Dean, Commandant, Director of Admissions, and the USMA Chief Surgeon, serve as voting members of the Academic Board, the senior decision-making body at West Point. All proposed change strategies must be approved by the members of the Academic Board prior to implementation.

Twenty-three senior military faculty hold appointments as Professor, USMA. These faculty are appointed by and serve at the pleasure of the President and Congress of the United States. These include the Dean, the 13 department heads, the Vice Dean for Education, the Master of the Sword (head of the Department of Physical Education), and seven deputy department heads (based largely on department size and historical precedent). The Vice Dean for Education serves as the Executive Secretary for the Academic Board, a non-voting position. All of these individuals are military officers and hold a rank of colonel or higher.

The Dean meets regularly and in a formal context, with the 15 department heads (or their appointed representatives) at the General Committee. All matters concerning the academic program, including curricular change, assessment, accreditation, or the management of cadet time, are formally discussed at this level. Proposed change strategies that are approved by this committee are forwarded to the Academic Board for deliberation and approval. The Curriculum and Assessment Steering Committees are standing bodies of faculty, appointed by the Dean, to review and offer recommendations to the General Committee. Both the Curriculum and Assessment Steering Committees are composed of military and civilian faculty. The Dean also receives input from the Faculty Council, an advisory body comprised of all faculty who hold the rank of associate or full professor. This council advises the Dean on several matters, to include ethics, the library, classroom technology, teaching effectiveness, laboratory resources, and faculty development.

Professional Development

Preparing faculty for the challenges they are likely to confront in the classroom requires a considerable focus on professional development. Approximately two thirds of the faculty are rotating military faculty. Of these, approximately one-third have arrived at the Military Academy fresh from a graduate program of study. Beyond the confines of their military experiences, they have little experience with formal classroom instruction. Therefore, the senior military and civilian faculty in the academic departments prepare and administer extensive faculty development workshops, which last from four-to-six weeks in duration and are offered each summer prior to the start of the academic year. These workshops focus exclusively on teaching and subject matter content in the core courses of the curriculum (primarily representing the first two years of college course work for cadets at the Military Academy). All new faculty, to include both military and civilians, are required to attend their department's workshops.

The core course material is organized by lesson. Each new instructor is issued a detailed course guide and accompanying textbooks. The course guides have been written and revised by those who have previously served as instructors in the course. The workshops are organized and administered by former instructors of the courses, the purpose of which is to ensure that all cadets receive the same breadth and depth of instruction in the core curriculum. The workshops have the effect of ensuring standardization of material across the core curriculum, provide a tremendous support structure for first-time instructors, and socialize new faculty to the West Point culture.

Professional development occurs in other venues throughout West Point. Insofar as the primary focus of the Military Academy is on cadet development, faculty are expected to work with cadets both in and beyond the classroom. Indeed faculty promotion places primacy on such activity. In addition to teaching excellence, faculty are expected to participate with cadets in extracurricular activities such as academic clubs (debate team) or athletics (varsity or club sports).

In addition, faculty are expected to contribute to their fields through publication in respected disciplinary outlets and offer assistance to colleagues through the development of collegial support structures (e.g., collaborative research or teaching teams).

Managing Change Strategies: USMA's Implementation of a Comprehensive Assessment Plan

In preparation for the 1989 reaccreditation review by the Commission on Higher Education of the Middle States Association of Colleges and Schools (MSCHE), the Military Academy's internal self-study acknowledged that the demands on cadet time made it difficult for West Point to achieve excellence in the academic program (United States Military Academy 1988). The 1989 MSCHE team agreed with this self-assessment and encouraged USMA officials to develop a mechanism that would allow for the integration of the Military Academy's three programs–academic, military, physicalówithin the institution's more comprehensive framework on leadership (United States Military Academy 1989). Essentially, MSCHE was asking the Military Academy to provide coherence both within and among its three programs; that is, MSCHE was recommending that West Point design and implement a comprehensive assessment plan, which would allow for systematic reviews, integration, and continuous improvement of the Military Academy's key curricular goals.

Because of the collaborative leadership context at the USMA, any proposed plan written solely by a member of the Superintendent's staff or the Institutional Research Branch of the Office of Policy Planning and Analysis would most certainly have failed because it would not have been collaboratively developed and approved by the key decision-makers at the Military Academy. To be approved and implemented, the plan would need to develop out of the academic program from deliberations among the 13 department heads. An approved plan would then be formally discussed at the General Committee and forwarded to the Academic Board for final deliberations. While the department heads approach any change strategy quite cautiously, several factors strengthened their resolve to incorporate a comprehensive assessment plan. First, MSCHE recommended that the Military Academy design an assessment framework to manage planned curricular change. Second, the engineering programs first received accreditation from ABET, the Accreditation Board for Engineering and Technology, in 1984. A comprehensive assessment plan would provide a framework for systematically managing the engineering programs. In addition, the Office of Policy Planning and Analysis was embroiled in an ongoing debate with Congressional staffers about the value of West Point compared to R.O.T.C. programs. While these debates have periodically resurfaced throughout the history of the Military Academy (see Ambrose 1966), the fact that they were revisiting this issue during the early 1990s was sufficient justification for reaffirming the linkages between the Army's needs and West Point's academic curriculum.

The task of managing student assessment within the context of the USMA was first reviewed by the Curriculum Committee during the 1990-1991 academic year. While members of this committee offered minor editorial changes to the goal statements associated with the academic program, they were unsuccessful in linking them to an assessment plan. The Dean created the Academic Assessment Committee in 1991 as a standing committee of military officers to review the linkages between assessment and curricular reform. Following three years of review and analysis, this committee produced a report in 1994 that outlined a model for the assessment of the academic program (United States Military Academy 1994;

see also the discussion in Forsythe and Keith 2003). The model was initially tested on one of the program goalsóthe engineering thought process. As the first engineering school in the United States (Ambrose 1965), senior leaders at the Military Academy have prided themselves on the significance of their engineering programs in the historical evolution of the United States during the 19th Century (Crackel 2002). An assessment of cadets' achievement of the engineering thought process goal therefore served as a meaningful context for the proposed assessment design.

During the academic year 1995-1996, the USMA witnessed a change in the position of the Dean. The new Dean placed assessment of the academic program as a top priority, seeking to build upon the work of his predecessor in this area. The recommendations offered by the Academic Assessment Committee in its 1994 report were favorably received by members of the General Committee. The report introduced the concept of a learning model–a description of the curricular structure necessary for cadets to achieve the goal, the process through which cadets gradually develop during the four year experience in pursuit of the goal, and the content to which cadets will be exposed during this structured process–with a focus on the engineering thought process goal. Subsequent development of learning models for the remaining goals was assigned to the members of the Assessment Steering Committee–a new working group of five department heads who designed the learning models for six program goals, including the engineering thought process, math, science, and technology, communication, understanding human behavior, historical perspective and cultural perspective. The Dean's strategy in assigning responsibility of this work to a subset of department heads emphasized the importance of the work and enhanced the legitimacy of their products. They completed this work during the 1995-1996 academic year.

During the spring of 1996, the Dean secured approval to

create a new administrative position on his staff for an assistant dean for academic assessment. He requested that the person hired for this position be a civilian with extensive experience in the assessment of higher educational programs. This action ensured that assessment would become a major priority for the Dean. The person hired for this position offered an outsider's review of the assessment model and data collection strategies. By the Spring term of 1997, considerable refinements occurred in several data collection strategies: the senior survey was overhauled to more closely align it with the revised goal statements and improve its methodological validity. In addition, new surveys were developed to obtain feedback from freshmen, graduates, and employers, which were comparable in scope to the revised senior survey. Moreover, focus group interviews were conducted with former battalion commanders located at the Army War College, which provided in-depth observations of graduates' strengths and weaknesses with respect to the corresponding goals. These data collection strategies have been in continual use since 1997, providing decision-makers at the Military Academy with longitudinal evidence of cadets' goal achievement.

By 1998, the learning models of the nine program goals received approval from the General Committee and Academic Board. These were published in the Dean's operational concept document, Educating Army Leaders for the 21st Century (United States Military Academy 1998) and are listed in Table 1. Department heads, now comfortable with the structure of this work, agreed to relinquish direct involvement of the implementation and assessment strategies to their senior faculty. Goal Teams were created for each of the nine goals and chaired by a senior faculty member who represented someone other than a department head. Each of these teams consisted of an average of eight faculty members. The teams were responsible for assessing the implementation and outcomes of the goals. Moreover, membership on the Assessment Steering Committee shifted from department heads to Goal Team chairs. Faculty were now fully engaged in the curriculum design and assessment process at West Point; department heads and senior administrators nonetheless retained veto power over the recommendations of this work through the General Committee and Academic Board.

During the 1999-2000 academic year, the Superintendent and the Secretary of the Army called for a review of the academic curriculum to ensure that the Military Academy was preparing cadets for the social challenges that they were likely to encounter throughout their Army careers. In particular, the Superintendent reiterated concerns voiced by the Secretary of the Army that USMA graduates may not have sufficient

Table 1: Goals of the USMA Academic Program

Graduates anticipate and respond effectively to the uncertainties of a changing technological, social, political, and economic world.

Upon achieving this overarching goal, graduates can:

- think and act creatively,
- recognize moral issues and apply ethical considerations in decision-making,
- listen, read, speak, and write effectively,
- demonstrate the capability and desire to pursue progressive and continued intellectual development,

and demonstrate proficiency in six domains of knowledge:

- Engineering and Technology
- Math and Science
- Information Technology
- Historical Perspective
- Cultural Perspective
- Understanding Human Behavior

Table 2: What Graduates Can Do: Academic Program Goals by Data Sources

Academic Program Goal Performance	4th Class ('00-'05)	1st Class '(97-'02)	Graduates ('96-'98)	Commanders ('96- 98)
Moral Awareness	4.36	4.47	4.80	4.58
Continued Education	4.26	4.47	4.57	4.56
Creativity	4.14	4.32	4.54	4.38
Communication	4.12	4.39	4.47	4.33
Cultural Perspective	4.21	4.33	4.53	4.42
Historical Perspective	4.10	4.24	4.35	4.22
Understanding Human Behavior	4.02	4.16	4.42	4.24
Math-Science-Technology	3.87	4.00	4.40	4.49
Engineering Thought Process	3.91	4.28	4.15	4.26
Intellectual Foundation	4.15	4.35	4.48	4.40
Number of Cases	4,909	1,992	1,290	679

Means are based on a 5-1 scale, where 5 represents very confident, 4 indicates confident, 3 equals somewhat confident, 2 indicates not very confident, and 1 represents not at all confident.

background in foreign cultures. This concern led to a wholescale review of the curriculum. The assessment data presented in Table 2, gathered to examine goal outcomes and used in conjunction with the operational concept document, showed decision-makers that graduates were indeed achieving the program's goals. If these were the correct goals, there was considerable evidence that cadets were achieving them. Instead of a undertaking wholescale changes to the curriculum, these findings provided the evidence necessary to reach a negotiated compromise with the Superintendent. The Academic Board agreed to refinements in some core coursework, particularly in the area of engineering, the creation of a tenth program goal in Information Technology, and acceptance of a recommendation that cadets be given opportunities, where available, to select an additional elective in foreign cultural studies. Without the assessment data, the outcome on the curriculum might have been much different. Indeed, the assessment data offered insights that the system could prevail over the preferences and personalities of senior leaders.

Following the curriculum review process, the ten program goals and the over-arching goal were re-examined and revised in light of available assessment data. The result was published in an updated operational concept paper, entitled, *Educating Future Army Officers in a Changing World* (United States Military Academy 2002). Perhaps more important than the publication of this document was the realization that the faculty claimed ownership of this strategic document and incorporated it into their faculty development workshops. New faculty were now being routinely socialized to recognize the operational concept as their overarching framework for the academic curriculum.

To further enrich the quality of these assessment efforts, the goal teams are presently looking at the use of embedded curricular indicators to directly assess cadet's course work. Faculty who serve on these goal teams are designing assess-

---

ment rubrics based on the their statements of what graduates can do, which were previously published in *Educating Future Army Officers in a Changing World* (see, e.g., Keith et al. 2002). The rubrics, upon completion, will be used to assess one or more course products–not so much for the grade received on the product but, rather, for the quality of the content associated with several important substantive domains of the respective goals.

Summary

The successful design and implementation of West Point's assessment plan required attention to several distinct issues. First, the proposed change strategy needed to be presented within the overarching vision of the institution. While proposed changes that challenge the established vision may succeed if the key decision-makers are in consensus with the new direction, one's understanding of the culture will be necessary if the faculty are to adopt the change and incorporate it into their established manner of doing business (Schein 1992). Second, senior administrators will need to be supportive of the change strategy; otherwise approval to change in the proposed direction may be tenuous. For example, grassroots efforts at initiating change strategies in colleges may have little chance of succeeding if the senior decision-makers are not in agreement with the proposed change. Third, collaboration among all key decision-makers is important if consensus is to be reached on the value of the proposed change strategy. At West Point, the three senior administrators comprising the leader team (Superintendent, Dean, and Commandant) constitute only 15 percent of those who serve on the Academic Board. To ensure success, department heads will need to be brought into a discussion of the proposed change strategy, with a majority reaching agreement on its merits. Without collaboration among key decision-makers, the proposed change strategy is not likely to be moved forward because it would potentially challenge the existing power structure. Fourth, implementation of the proposed change strategy will eventually require buy-in from all members of the faculty. Assessment is a local activity in that faculty must assess the work of students–senior administrators are not in a position to unilaterally accomplish this task. Therefore, full implementation of an assessment plan will require coordinated involvement by faculty, who must socialize their new and junior counterparts into recognizing the value of the proposed change. Absent attention to these four areas–vision, senior support, collaborative leadership, and professional development–the proposed assessment plan would likely gather dust on the proponent's shelf.

This essay has illustrated the importance of institutional context in managing proposed change strategies. To effect organizational change, proponents of proposed change strategies must recognize the institutional culture and prevailing power structure. Issues of great importance, such as an the design and implementation of an assessment plan, will necessarily need to be worked through the established leadership channels or risk being viewed as incompatible to the organization. In underscoring the importance of culture and context, our essay has emphasized the decision-making process within constrained parameters (structures). We contend that the process an institution experiences in its efforts to manage change strategies is as important as the final outcome. Regional accreditation boards may want to recommend that institutions document this decision-making process to the same extent that they describe their planned outcome. In this way, accreditation boards may be more readily able to identify those institutions that have sought to engage their culture in an effort to manage change strategies from those that have merely assigned a few staff members to write the outcomes of the assessment plan. Perhaps of greatest importance, though, is the experiential benefit accrued by the institution in its effort to work through this process of change. Clearly, an institution that manages change through a contextually appropriate system of assessment will enable its organizational participants to respond to current and future challenges within increasing sophistication and success.

References

Ambrose, S. E., (1966). *Duty, honor, country: A history of West Point.* Baltimore, MD: Johns Hopkins.

Austin, A. E. 1990. Faculty Cultures, Faculty Values, in *Assessing Academic Cultures and Climates.* William G. Tierney, ed. San Francisco: Jossey-Bass, pp. 61-74.

Banta, T. W., J. P. Lund, K. E. Black, and F. W. Oblander. 1996. *Assessment in Practice: Putting Principles to Work on College Campuses.* San Francisco: Jossey Bass.

Baenninger, M. and J. Morse. 2004. Accrediting Learning: Reflecting Student Learning in the New Standards of the Middle States Commission on Higher Education, in *Academic Contexts and Institutional Quality: Issues in Curriculum Design and Assessment.* Bruce Keith, editor. Stillwater, OK: New Forums Press.

Clark, B. 1985. Listening to the Professoriate. *Change. 17*(5): 36-43.

Crackel, T. J. 2002. *West Point: A Bicentennial History.* Lawrence, KS: University of Kansas Press.

Finkelstein, M. J. 2002. Tenure, in *Higher Education in the United States: An Encyclopedia, Volume 2.* James JF Forest and Kevin Kisner, editors. Santa Barbara, CA: ABC-CLIO, p. 666.

Forest, J. F. 2002. *I Prefer To Teach: An International Comparison of Faculty Preferences for Teaching over Research.* New York: Routledge Falmer.

Forsythe, G. B. and B. Keith. 2004. Assessing Program Effectiveness: Design and Implementation of a Comprehensive Assessment Plan, in *Academic Contexts and Institutional Quality: Issues in Curriculum Design and Assessment.* B. Keith, editor. Stillwater, OK: New Forums Press. 97-123.

Gouldner, A. W. 1957. Cosmopolitans and Locals: Toward an Analysis of Latent Social Roles. *Administrative Science Quarterly.* 2, 281-306.

Keith, B. 1996. The Context of Educational Opportunity: States and the Legislative Organization of Community College Systems. *American Journal of Education. 105*(1): 67-101.

Keith, B., J. LeBoeuf, M. J. Meese, J. C. Malinowski, M. Gallagher, S. Efflandt, J. Hurley, and C. Green. 2002. Assessing Students Understanding of Human Behavior: A Multi-Disciplinary Outcomes-Based Approach Toward the Design and Assessment of an Academic Program Goal. *Teaching Sociology. 30*(October):430-453.

Kezar, A. and P. D. Eckel. 2002. The Effect of Institutional Culture on Change Strategies in Higher Education: Universal Principles or Culturally Responsive Concepts? in *Journal of Higher Education. 73*(4): 435-460.

National Defense Authorization Act for Fiscal Year 1993, Pub. L. No. 102-484, Chapter 112, Section 2198.

Peterson, M. W. and M. G. Spencer. 1990. Understanding Academic Culture and Climate, in *Assessing Academic Cultures and Climates.* William G. Tierney, ed. San Francisco: Jossey-Bass, pp. 3-18.

Schein, E. H. 1992. *Organizational Culture and Leadership.* San Francisco: Jossey-Bass.

Tierney, W. G. 1991. Organizational Culture in Higher Education: Defining the Essentials. In *Organization and Governance in Higher Education.* Marvin W. Peterson, ed. Needham, MA: Ginn Press, pp. 126-139.

United States Military Academy. 1988. Institutional Self-Study: *A Report to the Commission on Higher Education of the Middle States Association of Colleges and Schools in Preparation for the 1989 Decennial Reaccreditation.* West Point, NY: United States Military Academy.

United States Military Academy. 1989. *Report to the Faculty, Administration, Superintendent, and Corps of Cadets of the United States Military Academy by an Evaluation Team Representing the Commission on Higher Education of the Middle States Association of Colleges and Schools.* West Point, NY: United States Military Academy.

United States Military Academy. 1993. *West Point 2002 and Beyond: Strategic Guidance for the United States Military Academy.* West Point, NY: United States Military Academy.

United States Military Academy. 1994. *Final Report of the Academic Assessment Committee.* Office of the Dean. West Point, NY: United States Military Academy.

United States Military Academy. 1998. *Educating Army Leaders for the 21st Century.* Office of the Dean. West Point, NY: United States Military Academy.

United States Military Academy. 2002. *Educating Future Army Officers for a Changing World.* Office of the Dean. West Point, NY: United States Military Academy.

Bruce Keith is professor and associate dean for academic affairs; **James J. F. Forest** is assistant professor and assistant dean for academic assessment. Both are located at the United States Military Academy, West Point, Ny.

Fostering Faculty Leadership in the Institutional Assessment Process

Armand S. La Potin and **Carolyn J. Haessig**
State University of New York – Oneont

Public regulatory and funding agencies, private foundations, and accrediting groups, are increasingly emphasizing accountability in higher education. Colleges and universities must demonstrate that they are doing what they claim to be doing. Consequently, they are expected to assess continuously the major goals incorporated in their institutional mission. Specifically, the current focus is on assessing "outcomes" of student learning and on "closing the loop." Assessment of student learning outcomes, which is part of overall institutional assessment, is the process for determining if students are accomplishing what faculty have concluded they should know, value and be able to do (the outcomes) as a result of their education. "Closing the loop" is a term used frequently to refer to how the findings of assessment activities are utilized in planning, so that the planning, teaching, assessing cycle is complete.

Although a diminishing number of faculty question the value of assessment or doubt its necessity, many who oppose it fear losing control of instruction. Consequently, it is important to show them how assessment can and should be part of instruction, and that they have a significant role to play as stakeholders.

Other faculty object to outcomes based assessment on philosophical grounds, perceiving that a pedagogical emphasis would subsume discipline-oriented concepts. But, even among those who are receptive to assessment, many were unfamiliar with how to assess outcomes, having yet to participate fully in the process.

The challenges facing campus leaders then, are formidable and amount to a major change in institutional culture. Such was the situation in the Spring of 1997, at SUNY College at Oneonta, a public, four-year college that offers a wide variety of bachelors and masters degree programs in either liberal arts and sciences or in selected professional fields. The College's deadline for submitting a Five-Year Periodic Re-

Figure 1: Definition of Assessment Terms

Student learning outcomes - descriptions of what academic departments intend for students to know, understand, or do when they have completed their general education core and degree programs.

Student personal development outcomes - descriptions of what professional staff intend for students to acquire in character development to make them responsible citizens in a multi-cultural society.

Programmatic goals - general statements of desired outcomes, such as student retention, derived from the Comprehensive College Plan.

view Report to the Middle States Commission on Higher Education Association (MSCHE) was June of 1998.

Accrediting agencies, including MSCHE mandated that institutions of higher learning demonstrate that they are undertaking institutional assessment; utilizing their findings in campus-wide planning, and specifically involving faculty in the articulation and assessment of student learning outcomes. Consequently, Oneonta's assessment efforts were designed to include: 1). Drafting an institutional assessment plan; 2). organizing workshops on the assessment of student outcomes for faculty and staff; 3). determining the format for assessment reports; 4). Preparing assessment reports; and, 5). Monitoring on-going campus assessment activities.

Their publications also made clear that the assessment process was very important. Adherence to process, is crucial in achieving meaningful findings from assessment activities that can be used in institutional planning, and initiatives that enhance faculty involvement at all stages of assessment are essential for success. Since faculty teach disciplinary course concepts that they articulate, assessment of student learning must be initiated and should be directed by faculty. Processes must be formulated that provide a base for the development of future faculty assessment leaders by enhancing faculty *ownership*. Consequently, the process used to garner broad involvement in assessment and ultimately leadership initiatives is as important as the merit of the derived outcomes. To the extent that it affects the quality of future outcomes, the process may be more important than the initial outcomes.

Having decided upon these guiding premises that placed considerable value upon meaningful and broad-based faculty involvement, and recognizing that "involvement" meant major change to the institution's culture, the initial faculty leaders needed to choose a strategy for moving the campus forward in this phase of the institutional assessment process – the assessment of student outcomes. Faculty leaders opted to use John P. Kotter's Eight-Stage Process as described in his book *Leading Change* (1996). Although Kotter's study is oriented toward private "for profit" enterprises, his outline of both the challenges faced by companies in an increasingly competitive global environment as well as his strategies in addressing these challenges has relevance for institutions of higher learning. Administrative systems and channels of communication are often similar, and both share a predilection to venerate "institutional culture." Equally significant, Kotter presents his model in a clear and concise fashion. The accomplishment of the College's goals by faculty using these eight stages is described using a "case-study" approach.

Step 1. Establishing a sense of urgency regarding the need to do assessment

> *Establishing a sense of urgency is crucial to gaining needed cooperation. With complacency high, transformations usually go nowhere because few people are even interested in working on the change problem. (Page 36)*

Given that for reaccreditation, the College had to submit its Five Year Periodic Review Report to Middle States (MSCHE) by June of 1998, it was relatively easy to use this impending deadline to create a sense of urgency regarding the need to do assessment. Additionally, faculty clearly were aware from MSCHE publications and the content presented in their workshops that assessment of student learning outcomes was among the expectations to be met by those institutions undergoing review. Thus, the need to undertake the assessment of student learning outcomes expeditiously could clearly be connected to an expectation that the College had to meet in order to remain in business.

As may be the case for many institutions, this initial sense of urgency for accomplishing outcomes assessment for the

College's accreditation was further enhanced by the potential consequences of New York State's impending imposition of "performance indicators." This set of performance measures is designed to permit the State University of New York System to monitor the progress of campuses in meeting their own and System-wide goals. These measures are intended to evaluate the performance of a campus in achieving its mission objectives and as a component in the formula to allocate state appropriations. Clearly, the urgency was real; however, communicating it and using it to prompt action was yet to be accomplished. That was to be the next task for the guiding coalition.

Step 2. Creating the guiding coalition

> *A strong guiding coalition is always needed - one with the right composition, level of trust, and shared objective. (Page 52)*

Establishing the leadership core to guide the campus's assessment efforts was a critical factor in the success of the project and would come from the guiding coalition. The goal was to establish a team that individually and collectively had credibility among their peers, and who shared a commitment to the opportunities and benefits inherent in assessment, particularly assessment of student learning. Thus, the Assessment Task Force was formed. [Originally called the "MSCHE Assessment Task Force," its name was changed early in 1998 to reflect the College's commitment to the premise that assessment must be on-going.]

The Task Force included representatives from different institutional perspectives - teaching faculty (from humanities and professional areas), administrators (from academic affairs, student development, and administration and finance), and students. However, the College's administration selected two senior faculty to serve as chair and vice-chair of the Task

Force since much of the responsibility for developing and assessing student outcomes would rest with faculty. Both were tenured faculty who had demonstrated appropriate team-building and organizational skills in other areas and the ability to work together. One was from liberal arts and the other from professional studies. It was crucial that faculty be charged with directing and supporting the efforts of their peers because faculty can relate personally to instructional issues and concerns such as course loads and academic freedom. Equally important, from the outset the deans, though not members of the Task Force, were positioned as key players in the process to ensure that over-all progress would not be blocked by a few.

Several untenured faculty who had expertise and interests related to assessment were included as members of the Task Force. For example, one faculty was chosen because of her training and research in educational psychology and learning. Another was selected because she could see how assessment could be accomplished and be beneficial to hers and other fine arts disciplines. A third member was included because he could identify issues likely to be common to those teaching sciences and other applied courses. As a reflection of the administration's clear understanding that assessment impacts all members of the campus community and therefore, all must be included in its design, the Task Force included two talented and dedicated undergraduate students. Initially then, the Task Force began formulating a vision and strategy for over-all assessment at the College and for the assessment of student outcomes in particular.

Step 3. Developing a vision & strategy

Without a good vision, a clever strategy or a logical plan can rarely inspire the kind of action needed to produce major change. *(Page 71)*

The Task Force began its work by formulating a set of "guiding premises" that should be followed in undertaking the assessment of student outcomes. These premises included a rationale for conducting student outcomes assessment, a description of when assessment would be conducted, who would conduct it and how the information would be used. In drafting the "guiding premises," Task Force members wanted to establish the importance of the College's linkages between student outcomes and institutional mission, and student outcomes assessment data with programmatic improvement through internal planning processes. The learning outcomes

Figure 2: Underlying Premises in the Formulation of Oneonta's Institutional Assessment Plan

1. Student outcomes are the primary focus for an assessment plan.
2. Student outcomes must be an outgrowth of the College Mission Statement.
3. Many constituencies of the College play an important role in the achievement of student outcomes.
4. Many student learning experiences occur outside the classroom.
5. Institutional assessment must enhance the effectiveness of the institutional planning process.
6. Existing data will be utilized in our institutional assessment where applicable.
7. Individual units will be encouraged to conduct their own assessment.
8. Assessment information will be utilized for programmatic improvement and accountability.

identified by the faculty are part of broader institutional goals and the assessment of these outcomes can lead to meaningful institutional changes. Thus, the "vision" is that the College is dedicated to continuous programmatic improvement, and the "strategy" is to have direct and on-going faculty involvement in the assessment process to achieve it.

With the vision and strategy in mind, the Task Force began its work drafting an institutional assessment plan (IAP). From the College's Mission Statement and Comprehensive College Plan, a series of action statements to achieve mission goals, the Task Force identified eight "Educational Components" to serve as focal points for organizing College-wide assessment activities. These "Educational Components" are: Academic Majors, General Education, Student Development, Information Literacy, Basic Skills, Student Services, Human Resources, and Facilities.

Step 4. Communicating the vision

... the real power of a vision is unleashed only when most of those involved in an enterprise or activity have a common understanding of its goals and direction. (Page 85)

Once the IAP was drafted, it was widely disseminated to members of the College community, and numerous hearings were held to answer questions about the plan and to receive comments. Throughout the consideration of the IAP, both process and product were emphasized.

It was essential that all concerned with the College had ample opportunity to question and react to the IAP before it was finalized. All hearings were open to the entire campus community, and the times were varied to accommodate different faculty and staff schedules. The Task Force also extended personal invitations to key members of the campus community, e.g. the presidents of the Student Association and the College Senate as well as members of the College Council, the local governance body.

As the IAP was being publicly reviewed by the campus community and eventually approved with minor revisions, the Task Force began developing expectations for faculty and staff with regard to student outcomes. These were to be articulated and subsequently assessed for both learning and personal development (see Figure 1). Expectations for the assessment of student outcomes were derived from information gathered at assessment workshops and conferences, such as those sponsored by MSCHE and the American Association for Higher Education.

The Task Force devised a workshop format and pertinent materials that were used to standardize the reporting of assessment activities and data across the campus. The final format selected for reporting was a two-page report that each program would submit annually. Materials, which included a PowerPoint slide series, were piloted with the chairs of academic departments. Task Force members, most of whom attended this session, field questions, shared examples of assessment activities and results from other colleges (obtained through web-sites), and addressed concerns. Subsequently, the Task Force revised the materials and the presentation based upon the suggestions of this group. Ultimately, workshop sessions for all faculty and select staff were structured as a "grass-roots" approach - program faculty or support staff working together and across programs to:

- review or establish their student outcomes;
- develop within a five-year period a time-line for assessing all of them;
- identify relevant learning experiences expected to result in the student's developing the competency;
- develop or locate means of assessing student learning; and

- identify how the results of the assessment would be used to improve instruction.

Task Force members presented the assessment workshop to faculty and staff six times during September and October. Faculty from majors and programs were asked to come together to the extent that their schedules permitted. Each workshop was two hours in length and was followed by a buffet dinner and social time for participants.

Step 5. Empowering broad-based action

... The idea of helping more people to become more powerful is important. (Page 101)

Faculty leaders utilized several techniques to encourage the active participation of a wide cross-section of their colleagues. The Task Force itself was broad-based and it modeled inclusiveness by managing the assessment workshops as a team, from planning to the actual delivery of the PowerPoint presentations. Junior faculty on the Task Force were encouraged to test their collegial leadership skills. Faculty who had attended an assessment workshop as a group were encouraged to maintain and expand their collaborative efforts. The workshops, subsequent one-to-one training, attendance at external assessment conferences, access to websites, and rotating membership on the Task Force were used to build concentric circles of support for the process.

Task Force leaders knew that at other campuses where initial participation in assessment was mandated, faculty commitment to assessment was low. At Oneonta, workshop attendance by faculty was voluntary, and only about 35% of full-time faculty participated in a session. Few initially agreed to attend a workshop with a high degree of enthusiasm. However, several faculty who were passive at the beginning of the two-hour workshop were "converted" enthusiasts at the end. One convert, the chair of a large department, soon began to embrace assessment and to encourage other faculty to do the same.

As more faculty learned about the assessment process, an increasing number became committed to if not entirely enthusiastic about it. Consequently, workshop attendance was only a first step, and not necessarily the route that each eventual participant would follow. Hence, that only 35% of all full-time faculty attended a workshop session was not a major issue.

Participation in external workshops also proved invaluable in empowering broad-based action. The College's administration funded three separate faculty teams to attend external "hands-on" assessment workshops or conferences sponsored by Alverno College, the American Association for Higher Education, and the MSCHE. Task Force members suggested colleagues who might benefit from attending such sessions. Participants were both tenured and untenured, represented all faculty ranks and disciplines, and varying levels of initial commitment to assessment. In retrospect, selecting those not previously identified as assessment enthusiasts proved to be an advantage, for it enhanced their credibility with other initially passive colleagues.

Access to web-sites from other colleges and universities proved especially valuable in enhancing support for the assessment process. Information available on the worldwide web includes various institutions' assessment plans, examples of programmatic assessment reports and secondary assessment sources. Some schools use their reports and findings as a recruitment tool to publicize their programs. Access to these sources is often critical at the point where faculty become intellectually curious about the process. At that stage, it is comforting for them to know how colleges with similar programs (and often similar disciplinary learning outcomes) assess them. When faculty move beyond intellectual curiosity, web-sites provide technical assistance in formulating assessment tools to measure learning outcomes. These sites have been used by "converts" to show their more passive colleagues that even "reputable" institutions of higher learning are constructively undergoing programmatic assessment. Rotating membership on the Task Force is broadening the base of support for the assessment process. Scheduling changes and faculty workloads precluded a consistent Task Force membership from one semester to another. "New blood" joined the group when it transitioned from the "MSCHE Assessment Task Force" to the present "Outcomes Assessment Task Force." Most of those who left the group remain committed to the process and continue to work with their colleagues. Their successors in the group are positioned to acquire the knowledge and skills to serve as peer models.

Step 6. Generating short-term wins

> *Major changes take time....Running a transformation effort without serious attention to short-term wins is extremely risky. (Page 119)*

Demonstrating immediate (though often limited) success is a strong motivating factor for people to pursue a course of action or lead others. Thus, when by the Spring of 1998 a few departments had completed the assessment of at least one of their articulated student learning outcomes, obtained feedback and formulated several recommendations for programmatic improvement, Task Force members decided to showcase these successes. With the department's permission, Task Force members presented and praised those that were positive examples at a meeting attended by department chairs.

Step 7. Consolidating gains and produce more change

> *Major change often takes a long time.... many forces can stall the process far short of the finish line... Short term wins are essential to keep momentum going but the celebration of these wins can be lethal if urgency is lost.* *(Page 132)*

As this is being written in the late Fall, 1998 semester, some of the preliminary findings from the programmatic assessment of student outcomes are being reviewed by the Future Directions Committee. This group, consisting of college constituencies similar to those of the Assessment Task Force, was formed following the implementation of the College's revised mission statement in 1991. It is charged with monitoring the efficacy of broad institutional goals, and with formulating specific action plans (The "Comprehensive College Plan") to achieve them. The Task Force plans to work closely with the Future Directions Committee to facilitate "closing the loop" in the assessment process.

Step 8. Anchoring new approaches in the culture

> *New practices (must) grow deep roots, ones that (sink) down into the core culture or (are) strong enough to replace it.* *(Page 147)*

As a consequence of both on-going external forces pressing for accountability in higher education and a growing recognition among institutional faculty that they can take the lead in the assessment process, early signs of a cultural shift are evident. The transition from an MSCHE Task Force charged exclusively with the preparation of the College's Five Year Periodic Review Report to an Outcomes Assessment Task Force, a permanent group to facilitate and monitor institutional assessment, created an institutional recognition that assessment is here to stay. Future workshops planned by the Task Force will acculturate new faculty and assist all instructional staff in refining the process of assessing their student learning outcomes. Significantly, as a consequence of the Task Force's efforts over the last year and a half and its work in the future, the College has a growing core of motivated and enthusiastic faculty leaders to guide the assessment process.

References

Kotter, J. P. (1996). *Leading Change,* Boston, MA: Harvard Business School Press.

Armand S. La Potin is emeritus professor of history at SUNY-Oneont.

Carolyn J. Haessig is professor of human ecology at SUNY-Oneont.

Accrediting Learning

MaryAnn Baenninger and **Jean Avnet Morse**
Middle States Commission on Higher Education

Institutional accreditors have been enhancing their emphasis on defining and assessing student learning in an effort to help faculty to design curricula, students to learn more effectively, and the public to understand the goals and results of higher education. This reflects a general transition in institutional accreditation towards emphasizing the importance of results while decreasing the emphasis on measuring resources.

This chapter explores how this emphasis has translated into revised accreditation standards, greater support for institutions seeking to enhance their student learning assessment programs, and focused training for administrators, faculty, and evaluators on how to lead, conduct, and evaluate campus assessment activities. The chapter focuses on the accreditation standards and activities of the Middle States Commission on Higher Education (MSCHE), but much of what is discussed in this chapter applies, at least in a general way, to the other seven regional accreditation Commissions across the United States.

Some of the topics we address in this chapter will be: What do accreditors expect, and why? What constitutes a plan for the assessment of student learning? What are some of the basic issues and concepts involved in the assessment of student learning? How is the assessment of student learning linked with overall institutional assessment? What kinds of resources do accreditors provide for their institutions in the area of student learning? How does the assessment of student learning relate to curricular design?

Other sections of this chapter address: the role of regional accreditation in higher education in the United States; the newly revised accreditation standards of the MSCHE, with an emphasis on how new accreditation standards represent a shift in thinking and values by the accreditation community in general; general characteristics of effective student learning assessment plans; developing learning goals and choosing assessment methods; and combining institutional assessment with assessment of student learning.

What is the Role of Accreditation?

Institutional regional accreditation is a voluntary process. Accredited institutions choose to be members and thus choose to demonstrate to their peers in the higher education community, and to the public, that they meet certain mutually agreed upon standards. The standards themselves are developed, revised, and approved by the membership. Contrary to common belief, regional accreditation is not governmental. All of the regional accrediting organizations in the United States undergo a cyclical review process in order to maintain recognition with the U. S. Department of Education. Such recognition transfers some of the "gate-keeping" power of the federal government to the accrediting Commissions in a way that is helpful to institutions. For instance, students from institutions accredited by recognized regional accreditors are eligible for federal financial aid. Thus, while regional accrediting agencies are non-governmental organizations, the federal government accepts their judgments of quality as a proxy for its own. Certain states and specialized accreditors also require regional accreditation.

There are three forms of higher education accreditation in the United States. Regional accrediting commissions, such as the MSCHE, accredit institutions. Professional program or disciplinary accreditors, such as ABET (Accreditation Board for Engineering and Technology) and NCATE (National Council for Accreditation of Teacher Education) accredit programs or schools, colleges, and departments (e.g. education departments). National accreditors, such as DETC (Distance Education and Training Council), accredit specific subject matter areas nationally. In addition, most states also engage in some form of statewide process designed to ensure quality.

How Accreditation Works: Standards and Processes

All of the regional accrediting organizations publish standards and processes for the accreditation of member institutions. MSCHE's fourteen standards are entitled *Characteristics of Excellence in Higher Education* and were most recently revised in 2002.

Their revision was accomplished through broad and diverse participation of the Commission's member institutions and with input from students, alumni, legislators, business leaders, federal and state quality assurance agencies, and national experts. Five task forces included representatives of every category of member institution: public and private; two-year and four-year; undergraduate, master's, and doctorate granting; non-profit and for-profit; secular and faith-based. The task forces led the revision process with support from the Commission's professional staff. Presidents, administrators, faculty, and other institutional personnel participated. The draft *Characteristics of Excellence* (*Characteristics*) was reviewed in several meetings around the MSCHE region by several hundred administrators and faculty, and the Commission invited comment from every institution before the members voted on the standards. This inclusive process, involving large numbers of individuals from member institutions, typifies the processes by which MSCHE institutes change.

The MSCHE standards relate to all aspects of higher education institutions (See Figure 1) and are divided into two subsections: Institutional Context and Educational Effectiveness. Both subsections include "capstone" standards: Standard 7 relates to institutional assessment, and Standard 14 relates to the assessment of student learning.

Accreditation fulfills its functions by encouraging each institution to involve its entire community in examining itself and in setting its own plans for the future through a "self-study" process.

In light of the variety of forms of higher education in the United States, and the differences in size, prestige, financial resources, geographic location, form of control (public, private; non-profit, for-profit), it is a challenge to retain the unity of the higher education community by applying the same 14 standards to all institutions in the region. How, for instance, can one review a two-year technical community college using the same standards as one would use for a private research university?

One of the most striking features of regional accreditation is the ability to craft standards by which both of these institutions can be judged, without compromising the integrity of the standard, without "watering down" the standards until they are meaningless, and without making judgments about the comparative quality of one institution versus another. Regional accreditation accomplishes this by using each institution's self-defined mission as the context for applying the standards, by using peer review as the cornerstone of the evaluation process, and by focusing institutional assessment on both accountability and improvement.

Focus on mission. Through its emphasis on mission,

Figure 1: Middle States Commission on Higher Education Standards at a Glance

---

Institutional Context

Standard 1: Mission, Goals, and Objectives
    The institution's mission clearly defines its purpose within the context of higher education and explains whom the institution serves and what it intends to accomplish. The institution's stated goals and objectives, consistent with the aspirations and expectations of higher education, clearly specify how the institution will fulfill its mission. The mission, goals, and objectives are developed and recognized by the institution with its members and its governing body and are utilized to develop and shape its programs and practices and to evaluate its effectiveness.

Standard 2: Planning, Resource Allocation, and Institutional Renewal
    An institution conducts ongoing planning and resource allocation based on its mission and uses the results of its assessment activities for institutional renewal. Implementation and subsequent evaluation of the success of the strategic plan and resource allocation support the development and change necessary to improve and to maintain institutional quality.

Standard 3: Institutional Resources
    The human, financial, technical, physical facilities, and other resources necessary to achieve an institution's mission and goals are available and accessible. In the context of the institution's mission, the effective and efficient uses of the institutionís resources are analyzed as part of ongoing outcomes assessment.

Standard 4: Leadership and Governance
    The institution's system of governance clearly defines the roles of institutional constituencies in policy development and decision-making. The governance structure includes an active governing body with sufficient autonomy to assure institutional integrity and to fulfill its responsibilities of policy and resource development, consistent with the mission of the institution.

Figure 1 *(continued)*

Standard 5: Administration
   The institutionís administrative structure and services facilitate learning and research/scholarship, foster quality improvement, and support the institution's organization and governance.

Standard 6: Integrity
   In the conduct of its programs and activities involving the public and the constituencies it serves, the institution demonstrates adherence to ethical standards and its own stated policies, providing support to academic and intellectual freedom.

Standard 7: Institutional Assessment
   The institution has developed and implemented an assessment plan and process that evaluates its overall effectiveness in: achieving its mission and goals; implementing planning, resource allocation, and institutional renewal processes; using institutional resources efficiently; providing leadership and governance; providing administrative structures and services; demonstrating institutional integrity; and assuring that institutional processes and resources support appropriate learning and other outcomes for its students and graduates.

Educational Effectiveness

Standard 8: Student Admissions
   The institution seeks to admit students whose interests, goals, and abilities are congruent with its mission.

Standard 9: Student Support Services
   The institution provides student support services reasonably necessary to enable each student to achieve the institutionís goals for students.

Standard 10: Faculty
   The institution's instructlonal, research, and service programs are devised, developed, monitored, and supported by qualified professionals.

Figure 1 *(continued)*

Standard 11: Educational Offerings
     The institution's educational offerings display academic content, rigor, and coherence that are appropriate to its higher education mission. The institution identifies student learning goals and objectives, including knowledge and skills, for its educational offerings.

Standard 12: General Education
     The institution's curricula are designed so that students acquire and demonstrate college-level proficiency in general education and essential skills, including oral and written communication, scientific and quantitative reasoning, critical analysis and reasoning, technological competency, and information literacy.

Standard 13: Related Educational Activities
     Institutional programs or activities that are characterized by particular content, focus, location, mode of delivery, or sponsorship meet appropriate standards.

Standard 14: Assessment of Student Learning
     Assessment of student learning demonstrates that the institution's students have knowledge, skills, and competencies consistent with institutional goals and that students at graduation have achieved appropriate higher education goals.

MSCHE sets standards that are at once universal and uniquely adaptable to a specific institution. Institutional mission is the lens through which the Commission and its evaluators apply *Characteristics*. Different institutions can meet accreditation standards in different ways, because the judgment of whether the standards are fulfilled can be tailored to the case of each institution.

     For instance, *Characteristics* includes a standard on student admissions. That standard does not specify what types

---

of students an institution should admit, nor does it set enrollment goals. What the standard does require is that any given institution, "seeks to admit students whose interests, goals, and abilities are congruent with institutional mission." The student sought by the research university may be different from the one sought by the technical community college, but each has an obligation to choose students who are appropriate to its goals and who will have a reasonable opportunity for success.

Peer review. It is the peer review process that enables mission-related assessment to determine an institution's ability to meet the standards for accreditation. All regional accreditors use peers as evaluators. In Middle States, the Commission itself is composed of twenty-seven elected faculty, presidents, provosts, and other administrators from member institutions and four "public" members who represent the interests of the general public in the region.

Institutional peers serve as evaluators (readers and/or visitors) for the decennial on-site evaluation and for the periodic five-year evaluation, which are both based on written reports. Peer reviewers are selected from a large database maintained by MSCHE. Thus, when a public comprehensive university is evaluated, the team that visits the institution generally would be chaired by the president of a public-comprehensive university, and the team itself would be composed primarily of faculty and administrators from similar institutions in other states. Evaluators who lead and teach at a specific type of institution are best suited to judge whether another institution of that type meets the standards. Evaluators take their roles very seriously and express their commitment to higher education by volunteering to participate in this work-intensive but very rewarding process.

Improvement and accountability. Focusing on both improvement and accountability enables regional accreditation to ensure that diverse types of institutions that have different strengths and weaknesses meet the standards and continue to improve.

To accredit an institution, MSCHE must determine that the institution meets its accountability responsibilities to its students, to other stakeholders in the institutional community, and to the public at large. Thus, accreditation indicates, among other things, that an institution is fiscally responsible, that its students are learning, and that the degrees it is granting have public and personal value, although institutions may reach these goals differently.

In addition to its accountability function, accreditation serves a very important improvement function. MSCHE helps institutions to raise quality in areas such as planning, educational offerings, and student support services, with the ultimate goal of ensuring that students are learning. This focus on improvement means that different institutions may decide to devote fiscal and human resources to different areas. Expert peer reviewers can best offer recommendations and suggestions about how each institution can improve.

Providing public information. The institution's self-study and the report of the peer review visiting team are shared with the institution's community. MSCHE publishes a directory describing all accredited institutions and makes available to the public a "Statement of Accreditation Status" that describes all actions for a particular institution voted by the Commission during the preceding ten years. Information on student learning outcomes is made available by the institution to prospective students and to the institutional community. The institution is free to circulate all or part of its self-study and visiting team report as part of the information that it regularly provides to the public.

New MSCHE Standards: Assessment of Student Learning

The revised accreditation standards adopted by MSCHE in 2002 place less emphasis on "inputs," such as physical plant or staff size, and more emphasis on "outcomes," such as student learning and job placement. This is intended to allow each institution the freedom and time necessary to produce its desired results in a manner that is most effective for the institution and its students. Two distinctive features of the revised standards are the emphasis on information literacy and on student learning in general. Both of these efforts are reinforced by supportive publications and workshops.

General education and information literacy. The emphasis on "information literacy" in the standards has been increased. A graduate must be able to perform the functions of effective information access, evaluation, and application. Different types and sources of training and information access may be appropriate for different institutions.

The standards expand the "general education" requirements that are applicable to all institutions. They now provide that students must "acquire and demonstrate college-level proficiency in general education and essential skills, including oral and written communication, scientific and quantitative reasoning, critical analysis and reasoning, technological competency, and information literacy. They also specifically address distance learning and requirements for certificate and non-credit offerings (Standard 13).

Demonstrating student learning. The MSCHE standard on the assessment of student learning (Standard 14) requires that "[a]ssessment of student learning demonstrates that the institution's students have knowledge, skills, and competencies consistent with institutional goals and that students at graduation have achieved appropriate higher education goals (*Characteristics*, p. 50)." MSCHE affords institutions the freedom to determine both the specific learning goals for their students and the means by which those goals will be assessed. Standard 14 does require certain "fundamental elements" that MSCHE expects will characterize the assessment of student learning at all member institutions:

- Articulated expectations of student learning at various levels (institution, degree/program, course) that are consonant with the institution's mission, and with the standards of higher education and of the relevant disciplines;
- A plan that describes student learning assessment activities being undertaken by the institution, including the specific methods to be used to validate articulated student learning goals/objectives;
- Evidence that student learning assessment information is used to improve teaching and learning; and
- Documented use of student learning assessment information as part of institutional assessment (*Characteristics*, p. 52).

Each MSCHE institution may choose how to satisfy these fundamental elements. For example, the institution can use flexibility in defining student learning goals at different levels (institution, program, course), and it can select the levels at which assessment among those three tiers will occur. In addition, the institution may choose not to assess all of its learning goals every year, and it may choose to use samples of student performance rather than assessing each student.

Institutional mission will have a central role in determining the major learning goals that an institution selects for its students. An institution and its visiting evaluators may well ask, "Is the institution concerned with ensuring that students are broad knowledge in the liberal arts, or have technical training, or are provided with a religious and spiritual context for their education?" "Does it emphasize goals that can reflect the value added by the educational experience offered at the institution?"

There may be a significant overlap among the goals that colleges and universities define at the institutional, program, and course levels. Institutional level goals may be achieved, directly or cumulatively, at the program level. For example, an institutional goal may include writing skill, but the institution may choose to achieve this goal by assessing writingat the conclusion of sudy in each departmental program or major, and it may will assess this skill at the course level in a variety of courses.

The assessment methods used by institutions may vary at the course, program, and institutional level. What may be a meaningful assessment at one level may not be relevant or practical at another. For instance, discipline-based standardized tests may be appropriate measures of student learning at the program level, whereas grades, when appropriately, directly, and consistently tied to specific expected performance, may demonstrate learning at the course level.

Guidance and support. In order to provide guidance and support, MSCHE has published a handbook, *Student Learning Assessment: Options and Resources.* It also has created a companion website (www.msache.org) that provides further resources and links to real examples at institutions. The handbook and the website offer guidelines and advice on developing an assessment plan, defining goals for student learning, and choosing and creating measures to assess whether that learning has occurred.

In each case, the intention is to provide a framework for formulating the most useful inquiries about assessment, rather than to prescribe how an institution should conduct its own assessment activities. For example, instead of specifying the content of the institution's plan for the assessment of student learning, MSCHE provides a set of characteristics of effective assessment plans and a set of components typically found in good institutional assessment plans. *Student Learning Assessment* also provides help for faculty and administrators who are developing learning goals for their students or choosing means of assessing these goals. None of the suggestions or guidelines presented is unique to MSCHE; instead, they reflect current best practices in higher education. Nor do they provide an exhaustive body of information on assessment for institutions in other regions, but they can serve as a helpful basis for beginning assessment, regardless of the region in which the institution is located.

General Characterists of Effective Student Learning Assessment Plans

Good practices for creating student learning assessment plans are similar to those for creating overall institutional plans, and student learning assessment plans are often a part of the overall institutional plan. This section mentions only key planning practices that are especially relevant to student learning.

The plan acknowledges already existing assessment practices. Institutions are encouraged to avoid "starting from scratch." Most faculty members are already engaged in defining and assessing student learning as a fundamental part of teaching, many student affairs staff already assess their activities on a regular basis, and the institutional research office or person responsible for institutional research often already conducts surveys and collects data on a wide range of student outcomes. The ongoing assessment activities at the institution can serve as the basis for developing an assessment plan, and existing course syllabi may define learning goals that are linked to assessment at the course level.

Acknowledging existing assessment practices demonstrates that the work of faculty and staff is valued, recognizes the cultural context of the institution, and provides some internal models for assessment. The plan need not require immediate assessment of all learning; it can provide for the overall assessment system to be phased in over time. By using existing assessment, the institution can "start with success" to reinforce successful practices.

The plan draws on the institutional mission. Good practice in the assessment of student learning is characterized by a focus on mission. What the institutional community expects students to learn emerges from what the community perceives to be the institution's reason for being. For example, if an institution's mission includes graduating students with specific skills, then institutional learning goals and the means by which they are assessed should reflect this commitment.

The plan is aligned with the institutional assessment plan. *Characteristics* stresses assessment and self-reflection for all components of an institution, and the institution is expected to implement a coherent plan for assessing itself. The plan for the assessment of student learning is only one part of this plan, but it is a central one: the ultimate goal of assessment is for an institution to demonstrate that its students are learning and that it is providing the structure within which this learning can occur.

Results from student assessments at the class, program, and institutional level feed back to both academic and other sectors of the institution and provide data on whether departments and professors are successfully accomplishing their own goals. For example, if students do not demonstrate the level of information literacy consistent with the institution's mission, then those who develop its budget might reexamine whether there is sufficient funding for the library and for educational technology, whether the library is sufficiently staffed, and whether physical resources including books and computer hardware and software are available to students. Those assessing the curriculum might explore how information literacy skills could be embedded in courses that must be offered by the department in which the student majors or embedded in a separate general education course. Similarly, those assessing the curriculum would determine whether it addresses information literacy adequately.

The plan is created by a participatory process. One of the commonly cited barriers to developing an effective assessment program is the failure of faculty members to "buy in" to assessment. Whether this barrier is perceived or real, it is clear that assessment must be an open process, and that it must grow from a grass-roots commitment to students and be supported by effective leadership and adequate resources.

The plan is simple. In order for an assessment plan to be useful in improving student learning, it must be understandable and workable. MSCHE encourages each institution to focus on its most important goals and to create a plan that will energize, not stymie, the campus community.

The plan is systematic. A coherent and systematic plan that covers the full-range of programs and services related to student learning provides a strong foundation for the institution's assessment program. The plan should include multiple approaches to assessing student learning and should reflect continuity and coherence among levels of assessment. Such systematization prevents duplication and omission in student learning assessment and allows for careful use of resources, both fiscal and human.

The plan has a realistic timetable. Assessment is a long-term process that involves several stages and requires great effort. Therefore, the timetable for assessment should include reasonable amounts of time to complete each stage on a cyclical basis. In apportioning time for each phase of assessment, the plan should take into account the busy seasons and rhythms of the academic calendar, and it should include time in the cycle to effect improvements. Conversely, the plan should not be so "long term" that campus constituencies lose interest or fail to appreciate the efficacy of the assessment process.

The plan is supported by institutional resources. *Characteristics* specifies that the "human, financial, technical, physical facilities, and other resources necessary to achieve an institution's mission are available and accessible (Standard 3, p. 7)." The provision of resources for the assessment of student learning is important both for the implementation of the plan itself and for implementing recommendations made as a result of information gathered during assessment. Institutions should consider "earmarking" funds to improve student learning on the basis of assessment results. Each institution should ensure that the timing for reviewing assessment results and planning for changes meshes with the schedule for the institution's budget process. The whole assessment process will be compromised if faculty, staff, and students discover that there are not enough resources in the budget to implement recommendations related to student learning.

The plan addresses faculty and staff time. The most important resource that should be considered in the assessment of student learning is faculty and staff time. Many assessment efforts fail simply because assessment is viewed as an "add-on." Assessment-related work often is not considered in tenure and promotion decisions, and pedagogically related activity is undervalued on some campuses. The plan should address carefully whether time should be reassigned for faculty and staff members to plan and conduct assessment activities and for faculty development activities such as workshops and conferences. The hasty response that there is not enough money for reassigned time or for faculty development may be a costly one in the long run if it stalls assessment activities and generates negative reactions to assessment. However, it is reasonable to expect that the definition of learning goals and assessment of student learning will become less time-consuming as it becomes more familiar.

Components of an institutional plan for the assessment of student learning. In an effort to help institutions to develop a plan for the assessment of student learning, MSCHE has developed the following list of components common to most good assessment plans. Although institutions may choose to adopt these components for their plans, MSCHE does not require that they do. Institutions are encouraged to develop assessment plans that address these areas:

- A statement of institutional mission
- A description of the relationship among the institution's strategic plan, institutional assessment plan, and student learning assessment plan
- A general description of the plan and guiding principles regarding assessment practices on campus, including guiding principles for the development of departmental or programmatic assessment plans
- Articulated goals for student learning at the institutional level
- Assessment methods used to assess the attainment of those goals
- A process by which assessment results are used to improve student learning
- A process by which the institutional plan for the assessment of student learning is reviewed periodically
- A time line or cycle for enacting the assessment plan
- A delineation of responsibility for implementing and maintaining the plan
- A provision for funding and/or support for implementing the plan

Learning Goals

Learning at the institutional, program, and course levels. After adopting a plan for the assessment of student learning each institution should follow through by developing goals for student learning as part of the assessment plan, implementing meaningful methods for assessing whether those goals have been attained, and using the information gained in assessment to help revise programs and courses. Student learning occurs at the course, program, and institutional levels. In courses, a student may learn the particular content of one area of his or her major, learn about specific additional content, and learn how to apply that content to specific tasks. In a program, a student may learn how to present information related to content and how to place that content in a broader context. At the institutional level, the student may acquire complementary knowledge and skills such as critical thinking and information literacy, perhaps in a general education program.

For example, at the course level, a student may learn the theory and history of nursing practice or human anatomy and physiology. At the program level, the student may develop applied nursing skills in various practica throughout the program. At the institutional level, the student may learn, through a general education program, to be a critical thinker and an intelligent consumer of newly discovered information about physiology. Of course, none of the types of learning described here are mutually exclusive–critical thinking and information literacy are certainly learned in nursing courses and practica, different institutions will address teaching at different levels, and each student may integrate learning experiences at different points. Nevertheless, various learning goals are usually achieved primarily in one area of the student's education.

For this reason, MSCHE expects its member institutions to demonstrate that the institution has defined learning goals at each of these levels, and that there is a systematic–though not necessarily complicated or exhaustive–relationship among the goals at the three levels. For example, an institution should be able to demonstrate that its faculty members consider overall institutional goals when they are developing program and course goals and that they incorporate program goals when developing the content of their courses.

Of course, some institutional level goals will be attained through aggregate experiences at the program and course level, rather than through learning experiences at the institutional level. Therefore, the profile of where and how goals are achieved would vary with the nature and sophistication of each goal. For example, the ability to make ethical decisions may be an institutional goal–to be demonstrated by all students, regardless of major–but it may be achieved through a requirement that each major program demonstrates that opportunities to develop ethical skills are woven throughout the program. A familiar example of this approach is the "writing intensive" course offered within majors or programs to achieve the institutional-level goal that students write well.

Parallel to MSCHE's expectation that goals for student learning be defined at all three levels is the expectation that those goals will be assessed, through multiple means, at the appropriate level or levels. The institution may choose the level or levels at which it will assess learning. It may not be desirable for an institution to conduct all of its assessment of student learning at the course level, for an institution to assume that its assessment commitment is met because its instructors assign grades, or that summative institutional assessment always provides accurate and believable data.

The MSCHE handbook, *Student Learning Assessment: Options and Resources*, provides extensive information for institutions about developing learning goals, about the relationships among goals at the institutional, program, and course levels, and about evaluating and using various assessment tools. The following sections address important concepts that MSCHE conveys to its members in the handbook and accompanying website.

Focus on key learning outcomes. When developing

learning goals at any level, it is important to focus on key learning outcomes rather than creating a long list of subordinate or less universal goals that might be subsumed in the more important key outcome. For example, a key learning outcome at the institutional level might be for students to become global citizens. This goal is clearly more important than the subordinate goal that a student exhibit detailed knowledge of geography, although such knowledge also may be expected.

Focusing on key learning outcomes also means not focusing on goals that are unrelated to the institution's mission. A technical institution with a focus on the building trades is unlikely to specify preparation for doctoral programs as a key learning outcome. An institution that concentrates on a few centrally important goals at the institutional level and for each of its programs is more likely to achieve those goals and to assess learning effectively.

Widely agreed upon concepts. The goals that emerge as key learning outcomes should reflect widely agreed upon concepts, developed collaboratively, and representative of various constituencies, including students. Learning goals should never be the result of the idiosyncratic view of a small group, regardless of whether it appears to be a mainstream view or an unconventional one. Faculty, staff, and students will be more committed to the process of learning, and to the idea that they should account for what students learn, if goals are shared.

Communication. Although development of goals should occur through a broadly participatory process, it is equally important that there is communication of goals to all invested stakeholders. One danger that institutions face is the tendency to develop goals and put them on a shelf and fail to develop widespread "buy-in", as has happened often with plans for new general education programs in the last 20 years.

Meaningful goals. Goals for student learning should be

meaningful and not trivial. For example, goals that require students to memorize historical dates, be able to use a specific computer program, or spell correctly, are not useful if the student cannot analyze events in an historical context, master a set of heuristics involving the principles underlying all computer programs, or write a comprehensible paragraph. In developing goals, it is important for faculty and staff to consider which "subsidiary" skills will follow naturally as primary goals are attained.

Explicit goals. Although learning goals may be trivial if they are too specific, learning goals should be sufficiently explicit so that they can be commonly understood. A goal that students should learn to be "global citizens" may have a variety of meanings. Does being a global citizen mean being at home in a variety of cultures, speaking non-native languages proficiently, exhibiting a "social justice" orientation towards those less fortunate, demonstrating ecological responsibility, understanding global business practices, demonstrating geographical knowledge, or something else? None of these goals is trivial, but none is made explicit in the overarching goal of global citizenry.

Ways that learning goals can help students, faculty, staff, and the public. There are several reasons to ensure that learning goals are public and accessible for faculty, staff, students, and prospective students.

Students who are able to ascribe meaning and purpose to their learning will not only perform better in class, but they also will retain what they have learned and will be more likely to put it into practice. Prospective students can use available learning goals to help determine whether a particular major or institution is appropriate for them. For example, many psychology students choose their major because they "want to help people with their problems." Exposure to learning goals for the psychology program–which in some institutions may include emphasis on research methodology, statistical reasoning, cognitive and learning theory, social behavior, physiology and neuroscience, with comparatively little emphasis on clinical practice–may help a student decide against majoring in psychology. The availability of clear learning goals also helps students to give useful feedback to the instructor about whether intended instructional goals are met, rather than using student surveys or "popularity contests." They also can help students to understand successes and failures in their own class performance.

For faculty, clearly articulated and shared learning goals help to lend structure to course preparation and to aid in deciding what to include or exclude in an already compact course. The discipline of psychology provides another example. Typically, most psychology programs begin with a one- or two-semester survey of all areas of psychology. This course is difficult to teach because of the overwhelming quantity of material that must be covered, including approximately 15 subfields of psychology, many of which have become disciplines in their own right. If faculty members in a department have determined that the most important goal for the course is to teach the principles of psychology rather than the factual content (which can be attained fairly easily through a good textbook), then they can design the course around research methodology and hands-on experimentation, selecting examples from the various sub-disciplines to underscore the principles taught in the classroom. Without a clear learning goal of this type, students and faculty alike will trudge through the massive text without ensuring that any particular outcome is achieved, except perhaps to have the students' heads whirling with facts. Assessment of student learning will help faculty to determine whether their goals have been achieved by their approach.

Shared communication of learning goals helps faculty members in other ways. It is helpful for faculty to be familiar with the learning goals of other courses or other programs when developing goals for their own courses or program, because learning goals at the institutional and program levels often represent aggregates of, or connections between, learning goals at subordinate levels. In the case of "service courses", it is helpful for faculty who are teaching many students from other programs to know the learning goals of other programs in order to ensure that their course is meeting the needs of other programs.

The public benefits from the specificity of the learning goals and the clarity of the assessment results. Parents, legislators, taxpayers, and others have been demanding proven results for the increasingly high investments of time and money. The goal of improving assessment of student learning is to try to meet those needs without "homogenizing" higher education through required standardized testing. Everyone benefits from improved learning.

Evaluating Student Learning

Choosing assessment measures. In order for the assessment of student learning to be meaningful, the measures or assessment tools need to be valid, reliable, and useful in helping to institute change in programs or curricula. Instead of specifying which measures institutions should use, accreditors emphasize the choice of appropriate measures for each goal. The MSCHE handbook, *Student Learning Assessment: Options and Resources*, provides to the reader some general measurement and research concepts, offers some basic guidelines for choosing measures, and discusses various measurement techniques. The emphasis is placed on thoughtful and practical measurement, not on cumbersome, fastidiously controlled techniques. While adherence to some basic research concepts is important for the validity and reliability of measures used to assess student learning, those engaged in assessment practice are discouraged from practicing "methodolotry"–making the method more important than the assessment question. Two often discussed concepts pertaining to the assessment of learning goals are the distinction between direct and indirect measures and the appropriate use of qualitative and quantitative data.

Direct versus indirect measures. Direct measures of student learning (such as an examination, scores on a rubric, homework assignments) are those that demonstrate that specific learning has occurred. For a measure to be direct, it must reveal the content of a student's learning.[1] Direct measures alone, however, are results without explanations. Without some knowledge of the reasons why students have or have not learned, decisions about how to change a course or curriculum are uninformed.

Indirect measures focus on reasons why learning may or may not have occurred and on students' perceptions of their learning experience. Indirect measures can provide data for making decisions about how to change the learning environment to ensure better performance on direct measures of student learning in the future. For example, scores on a calculus midterm exam (direct measure) may reveal that most students have not mastered the material (e.g. 75% of students score 70% or lower). An indirect measure, such as a questionnaire about math anxiety and study habits, coupled with information about students' prior math courses (indirect measures), may reveal that students who performed poorly are not distributing their study time most effectively, or are experiencing high levels of math anxiety. This information can be used to help the instructor redesign the course–perhaps by

---

[1]A direct measure may or may not assess "value-added" learning; individual institutional, program, or course goals would determine whether the measure should demonstrate that students know more than they knew before they began the course of study. "Competency-based" goals would require that students achieve a certain level of performance.

Contexts for Learning

requiring smaller evaluations more frequently–thus reducing students' anxiety and forcing them to distribute their study time more evenly across the material. Direct and indirect measures of student learning are both valuable tools: direct measures are essential to demonstrate whether learning has occurred, and indirect measures are indispensable because they provide insights into how learning can be improved.

Qualitative and quantitative data. Two common and related misperceptions about assessment surround the use of quantitative and qualitative data. The first is that only quantitative data are meaningful because qualitative data cannot be analyzed. The second, its inverse, is that accreditors only value quantitative data, but that qualitative data are the only data available in some disciplines. Both arguments have been used to discourage outcomes assessment and both are shortsighted. The use of both qualitative and quantitative data should be encouraged when appropriate.

Measures that rely on quantitative data offer fast, easily comparable results, and scoring can often be accomplished electronically. If these measures are constructed properly, the numbers they yield can be meaningful representations of what students have learned, or their perceptions of what they have learned or experienced.

Qualitative data offer richness and an opportunity for subtle nuances to be expressed, either in the demonstration of learning (as in an essay exam[2]) or in the revelation of perceptions (as in a focus group). Again, the focus for accreditors, and MSCHE in particular, is on the use of the appropriate type of measure for the learning goal that is being assessed.

MSCHE also provides guidelines to help faculty members and staff choose appropriate assessment measures. These guidelines form the basis of a series of questions that can be

---

[2]Of course, narratives like those produced in response to essay questions can be scored quantitatively, but the raw data are qualitative.

Conclusion

Accreditation is shaping the national discussion about the quality of higher education by creating new standards that clarify the general scope and nature of student learning assessment. The method of using peers to evaluate each institution allows institutional accreditors to assure the quality of education without compromising the flexibility that has allowed American institutions of higher education to offer excellent education that suits the different missions of diverse types of public and private colleges and universities. Accrediting commissions offer support and training to their members in their effort to define, assess, and improve student learning.

If faculty, administrators, students, accreditors, and others cooperate in defining learning goals, measuring results effectively, and enacting constructive change, then the justifiable need of students and the public to understand the nature of learning and to be assured of its quality can be satisfied without resorting to less sophisticated, less flexible, and less useful assessment methods.

References

Middle States Commission on Higher Education (2002). *Characteristics of Excellence in Higher Education, Eligibility Requirements and Standards for Accreditation.* Philadelphia: Middle States Commission on Higher Education.

Middle States Commission on Higher Education (2003). *Student Learning Assessment: Options and Resources.* Philadelphia: Middle States Commission on Higher Education.

Mary Ann Baenninger is the Executive Associate Director of the Middle States Commission on Higher Education, Philadelphia, PA.

Jean Avnet Morse is the Executive Director of the Middle States Commission on Higher Education, Philadelphia, PA.

Index

A

AACSB Business Management Test 158
Academic Profile 46
Accountability 220
Accreditation Board for Engineering and Technology 187
ACT 79, 159
Active learners 125
Adelman, Clifford 3
Alverno College 209
Ambrose, Stephen 187
American Association for Higher Education 98, 209
American Chemical Society Exam 159
American Council on Education 71
Angelo, Thomas A. 107
Army War College 115, 189
Assessment-as-Process 6, 146
Assessment Blue Ribbon Committees 161
Assessment measures 235
Assessment model 97, 98, 126
Assessment of: Accounting 128; American History 120; American Literature 85; Arts and Humanities 49; Basic Skills 153; Biological and Physical Sciences 49; Biology 83, 135, 167; British Literature 85; Business 168; Chemistry 35, 167; Communication Skills 10, 48; Computer Science 167; Continued Educational Development 112; Creativity 112; Criminal Justice 170; Critical Thinking Skills 48; Cultural Awareness 48, 49, 120; Developmental Reading 40; Economics 169; Education 169; Engineering Design Projects 114; English Literature 168 English 39, 83, 85; General Education 46, 77, 132, 153; Historical Awareness 49, 110; History 83, 168; Independent Learning 48; Information Literacy 48, 49, 222; Learning Outcomes 53; Mathematics 4, 170; Math-Science-Technology 110; Moral Awareness 112; Music 168; Physics 167; Political Science 83, 169; Psychology 39, 169; Social Sciences 49; Sociology 83, 169; Speech 39; Student Learning 24, 125, 145, 146, 213, 222, 231, 235; Understanding Human Behavior 110; World History 120;
Assessment plan 30, 76, 119, 146, 173, 175, 178, 194, 206, 226
Astin, A. W. 107
Austin, Ann 176
Ayala, Frank 107

Contexts for Learning